The Smithsonian Treasury

AMERICAN QUILTS

Doris M. Bowman

NATIONAL MUSEUM OF AMERICAN HISTORY

Analysis of the Quilts by Joan Stephens

SMITHSONIAN INSTITUTION PRESS · WASHINGTON, D.C.

Produced in cooperation with the Book Development
Division, Smithsonian Institution Press.

All images copyright © Smithsonian Institution,
except as noted in the Acknowledgments.

A Gramercy Book
distributed by
Random House Value Publishing, Inc.
40 Engelhard Avenue
Avenel, New Jersey 07001

Manufactured in the United States of America

Library of Congress Cataloging-in-Publication Data
Bowman, Doris M.
American quilts / Doris M. Bowman ; analysis of the
quilts by Joan Stephens.
    p.   cm.—(The Smithsonian treasury)
"A Gramercy book."
ISBN 0-517-05952-5
1. Quilts—United States—Catalogs.   2. Quilts—
Washington (D.C.)—Catalogs.   3. National Museum of
American History—Catalogs.   I. Stephens,
Joan.   Analysis of the Quilts.   II. Title.   III. Series.
NK9112.L4   1991
746.9'7'0973074753—dc20   91-18638
                                                                CIP

8 7 6 5 4 3 2

CONTENTS

INTRODUCTION

QUILT . . . A cover or garment made by putting wool, cotton or other substance between two cloths and sewing them together, as beds covered with magnificent quilts.
AN AMERICAN DICTIONARY OF THE ENGLISH LANGUAGE
by Noah Webster, LL.D., New York, 1828

Today craft and art unite in a quilt. The art is usually obvious, in glorious patterns of stitches and colors, some regular and familiar, others riotous and new. The craft can be more difficult to detect. It lies in part in the quiltmaking itself—the patient labor of transforming cloth or scraps of fabric into something beautiful or useful, and often both. But the craft can also be measured in a quilter's terms, in the number of patches, the ingenuity of the quilt's construction, or even the number of stitches per inch.

Tradition and originality also meet in a quilt. Modern artists who have chosen quiltmaking as a means of expression have selected an inescapably traditional art. Because quilts are made at least in part by hand, they have an unbroken link to the past, when almost everything was handmade. American quiltmaking traditions remain a part of modern quilts, many of which are exciting and energetic variations on traditional themes.

Quilts appear today at auctions, county fairs, juried art competitions, and international exhibitions. They are the subjects of scholarly studies, evidence for historians of American art, the pride of the collector, and the investor's bet. Many quilts never spend a day on a bed; instead they decorate the walls of beautiful homes and offices of lawyers, doctors, and architects, and sell for thousands of dollars in the shops of London, Paris, Tokyo, and Milan. Quiltmaking has never been more popular in the United States than it is today, and the quilter's products are attracting an ever-widening audience.

The earliest quilts in America probably arrived with European settlers. The earliest quilts made in America were almost certainly pieced together from scraps of clothing and household fabrics. Unfortunately, no existing examples of seventeenth-century quilts have surfaced to offer clues to the materials and techniques of the day. Most of those early quilts were probably recycled in some way because of the necessity to use and re-use every available scrap of fabric.

The earliest surviving American quilts date from the eighteenth century. Although few in number, they offer important clues about their owners. The use of a single fabric for an entire quilt top, for example, was a luxury only a prosperous household could afford. Patchwork quilts proclaimed the thrift and determination of a quilter of modest means, or practical bent, not to waste the tiniest scrap, while at the same time creating a thing of beauty from the humblest sources.

Many quilts survive from the nineteenth century, when both time and materials to devote to the decorative aspects of quiltmaking became increasingly plentiful. One of these materials was chintz, a printed and sometimes glazed cotton. In *Recollections of a Housekeeper*, published in New York in 1834, Mrs. Clarissa Packard wrote, "Lyddy made two quilts of marvelous beauty. . . . To accomplish these chefs d'oeuvre I had seen several yards of good chintz destroyed." Miss Florence Hartley commented in the *Ladies' Hand Book of Fancy and Ornamental Work,* published in Philadelphia in 1859, "if, as we once knew a lady to do, you buy the finest, highest priced French chintz to cut up into inch pieces, it is not perhaps so great a saving as it would be to buy the quilt outright."

Even as some quilts began to proclaim their extravagance, practical quiltmaking endured. Miss Hartley observed, "In an economical point of view there is great saving in patchwork quilts, if they are made from pieces of cloth already in the house, which are useless for anything else." Since plain, utilitarian quilts were seldom saved or recorded in family papers, surviving nineteenth-century quilts give a fragmented overview of quiltmaking.

Until well into the nineteenth century, needlework was one of the few acceptable creative outlets for women. A few men made quilts, but most were made by women, and their creations enabled them to combine artistic expression and practicality. Every elaborate extravagance of design and painstaking labor could be justified by the sheer thrift of the endeavor. By displaying their quilts at fairs, women received recognition for their work and found inspirations in the other quilts exhibited.

Quiltmaking could also be a social ritual and an event, providing an opportunity for women to meet and talk as they created a valuable gift to celebrate a friendship or a special occasion. Frances Trollope, a British traveler in the United States, wrote in *Domestic Manners of the Americans,* published in London in 1832, "The ladies of the Union are great workers, and, among other enterprises of ingenious industry, they frequently fabricate patchwork quilts. When the external composition of one of these is completed, it is usual to call together their neighbours and friends to witness, and assist at the *quilting,* which is the completion of this elaborate work. The assemblings are called 'quilting frolics', and they are always solemnised with much good cheer and festivity."

A quilting frolic was also simply called a "quilting," or a "bee." And a woman could, of course, quilt alone. But a gathering of quilters often presents a special scene. Describing a work of art entitled *A Quilting Party in Western Virginia,* shown above, an unknown contributor to *Gleason's Pictorial Drawing-Room Companion,* published in Boston in 1854, wrote "The artist has presented for us . . . a characteristic and expressive picture of country life in Western Virginia. The scene represents a quilting party convened at the house of a villager to assist in this domestic labor unitedly. . . . Age and infancy, youth and maturity are here delineated, ease and

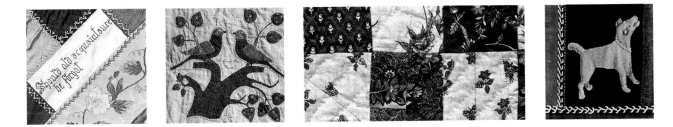

awkwardness, roughness and gentle refinement, just such a heterogeneous compound of life, as such social gatherings are composed of."

As if all these virtues of a quilt were not enough, quilts were also thought to play a part in the social redemption of women. According to Miss Hartley, "There is in this State, an institution for the reformation of girls who have been imprisoned for some crime; they are taught to sew neatly, and each one is allowed to exercise her taste and ingenuity in the manufacture of a patchwork quilt, which she is allowed to take away with her when she leaves. I have seen one hundred and fifty beds in this institution, each covered with a different pattern of patchwork quilt; some very tasteful and pretty, others not."

The national quilt collection is in the care of the Division of Textiles of the National Museum of American History. It had its beginnings in the 1890s when three late-eighteenth- and early-nineteenth-century quilts were donated to the Smithsonian by John Brenton Copp of Stonington, Connecticut. They were part of an extensive gift of household and costume items that had belonged to his family. The collection has now grown to more than three hundred quilts and unquilted tops and many quilt pieces and sections, most of them gifts, and many from the families of the quiltmakers.

This book presents a representative selection of quilts from the collection. It includes examples of many of the materials and techniques used by American quilters from the eighteenth century through the early twentieth century, as well as many of the types of quilts made.

The descriptions of the quilts include many technical terms. *Patchwork,* for example, is a term encompassing both piecing and appliqué, two methods of stitching pieces of fabric together to make quilt tops.

In *pieced work,* the scraps or cuttings of fabric are seamed or whipped together.

In *seaming,* two pieces of fabric, face sides together, are stitched parallel to and near the edges to be joined. All the stitching is done on the reverse side of the fabrics. The fabrics are separated out and flattened, leaving the seamed edges on the reverse side, and no stitches visible on the face side.

In *whipping,* the edges of the pieces to be joined are turned under, abutted, and stitches taken alternately through the folded edge of one piece to the folded edge of the other. These stitches, although often tiny, can be seen along the join line.

In the Copp family's Framed Center Quilt, on page 22, both whipping and seaming were utilized. The pieces in the quilt center are whipped together, while the border pieces are seamed.

In American quilts, *appliqué* usually refers to onlaid appliqué, the most common form used. The design shapes are cut out of fabric and stitched onto the surface of a contrasting background fabric.

In *reverse appliqué,* the positions of the pattern and background fabrics are reversed from those of onlaid. The silhouette of the pattern is cut out of the background fabric, and the openings are filled by applying a contrasting fabric from underneath.

In American quilts reverse appliqué was used far less often than onlaid, but museum collections have a few fine examples indentified as late eighteenth- or early nineteenth-century by their materials and patterns. The reverse appliqué quilt on page 17 is a rare dated example.

In *chintz appliqué,* the quilter cuts around the designs of printed fabrics and stitches

them to a background fabric. In his history of the textile industries of the United States, published in Cambridge, Massachusetts, in 1893, William Bagnall theorized that "The application of motifs cut from printed fabrics may have begun as a means of utilizing savable portions of beautiful chintzes so popular in the eighteenth century."

At times, appliquéd motifs were made three-dimensional by padding, usually with cotton fibers. This technique is known as *raised appliqué.* In the Palmer sisters' raised appliqué quilt, on page 60, cotton fibers were inserted under most of the raised appliquéd motifs through slashes in the ground fabric, while the strawberries in the border of Eliza Jane Baile's Bride's Quilt, page 50, appear to have been padded on the face of the background fabric as the strawberries were appliquéd. The flower stems in the Palmer quilt are made of green cotton fabric wrapped around rolls of white cotton fabric, giving them a raised and rounded appearance. The flowers of the Maryland Album Quilt, on page 53, have been raised by gathering folded strips of fabric and stitching them to the ground fabric of the quilt top.

Nineteenth-century American quilts are rich in examples of *stuffed and corded work,* in which additional padding raises the quilting designs for a low-relief sculptural effect. The extra stuffing, usually cotton fibers, was pushed into the pattern areas through small slits cut in the quilt lining or through spaces between its warps and wefts. A less common technique was to stitch the design to be raised through the quilt top, the filling, and a loosely woven cotton lining through which the stuffing was inserted. Then an outer layer would be added and the background quilting stitched through all the layers. Narrow channels in the design, such as flower stems, were sometimes padded by pulling cords or slightly twisted strands of fibers through them with the aid of a needle or bodkin.

A quilt is a fabric sandwich. The top and bottom layers surround an inner filling. Quilting stitches hold the several layers of the quilt together. In this book, quilts with tops made of a single kind of fabric are referred to as quilted counterpanes. Those quilts that have tops of plain fabrics depend on the quilting stitches for decoration, and the quilting pattern is often elaborate. In counterpanes with printed fabric tops, the printed pattern dominates the quilting pattern, which is usually much simpler.

THE PATCHWORK QUILT

There was a time when American housewives prided themselves on their neat and often elaborate patchwork quilts; and merry indeed were the "quilting-bees," when the women, young and old, married and single, used to gather at some neighbor's house to take a hand in the work. . . .

There are few parts of the country where this custom still lingers, cheap manufactures having superseded the necessity of this branch of domestic industry. Here and there may be found some old grandmother who still clings to the habits of her youthful days, and employs much of her time at the quilting-frame. . . . The next generation will know them only by tradition, and by such pictures as the one we give on this page.

Harper's Weekly, December 21, 1872

More than a century after this doleful prediction, American quilters have proved its author wrong. The current generation knows quilts by their artistry and abundance, as well as by their tradition, and the next generation will have a still richer tradition to discover.

Eve Van Cortlandt

The fine linen top of this white counterpane is decorated only with its quilting stitches. They trace a delicate pattern of flowers, feathery stems, and low open baskets that surround a central quatrefoil medallion. All are set off by a background of parallel lines just 1/8 inch apart.

The quilt was made by Eve Van Cortlandt and is one of the earliest dated American quilts in existence. The date, "1760," and her initials, "E V C," are embroidered on the quilt lining.

Eve was born on May 22, 1736, to Frederick Van Cortlandt and Francena Jay, both from families of wealthy New York landowners. She made her quilt for her dower chest while living in the family home, now a museum in Van Cortlandt Park in the Bronx. In 1761, Eve married the Honorable Henry White, a businessman and a member of the King's Council of the Royal Colony of New York. He became president of the New York Chamber of Commerce in 1772 and remained loyal to the King of England during the Revolution. When the British evacuated New York in 1783, Henry moved his family to England. In 1786, Eve returned to America as a widow, and died in 1836 at the age of one hundred.

QUILTED COUNTERPANE

Linen top. Cotton lining; initials embroidered in blue silk. Cotton fiber filling.   98 × 87 inches

RESIST-DYED QUILT

Cotton top. Linen lining. Wool fiber filling.   94 × 83 inches

The top of this quilt is of resist-dyed cotton that probably dates from the mid-eighteenth century. To obtain the pattern, a dye-resistant substance was applied to the area that was not to be colored. The fabric was then dipped in an indigo dye. To achieve the two shades of blue, the lighter blue was dyed first, then covered with the resist and the fabric was dipped again for the darker blue. The resist was then removed, leaving the background undyed.

The quilt is said to have been made by Clara Harrison of Middlebury, Connecticut. The patterned cotton was probably used originally for curtains and other bed furnishings and re-used in the quilt in the eighteenth century.

CHINTZ APPLIQUÉ QUILT TOP

Cotton.   63 × 63 inches

The center of this quilt was made by Mary Gorsuch Jessop, who was born in 1767 and married Charles Jessop when she was twenty-one years old. Until her death in 1832, Mary lived at Vaux Hall, the Jessop plantation in Baltimore, Maryland.

While Mary may have made the quilt center in the late eighteenth century, the appliqué of the triangular corner pieces is cut from an English chintz of about 1830, and may have been added by Mary's daughter-in-law, Cecelia.

The sixteen block-printed motifs applied to the center square are the work of John Hewson, one of the few eighteenth-century American textile printers who have been identified. Persuaded by Benjamin Franklin to leave England before the Revolutionary War, Hewson set up his printing works on the banks of the Delaware River near Philadelphia. There he worked with such skill and success that the British, who sought to eliminate competition for their products, posted a reward during the war for his body, dead or alive. He survived to demonstrate fabric-printing, aboard a float, in the Grand Federal Procession held on July 4, 1788, in Philadelphia to celebrate the adoption of the Constitution. William Bagnall wrote in his history of the textile industries of the United States, published in 1893, that, "President Washington was accustomed to point with patriotic pride to domestic fabrics worn by Mrs. Washington and printed at the works of . . . Hewson."

SMUGGLER'S QUILT

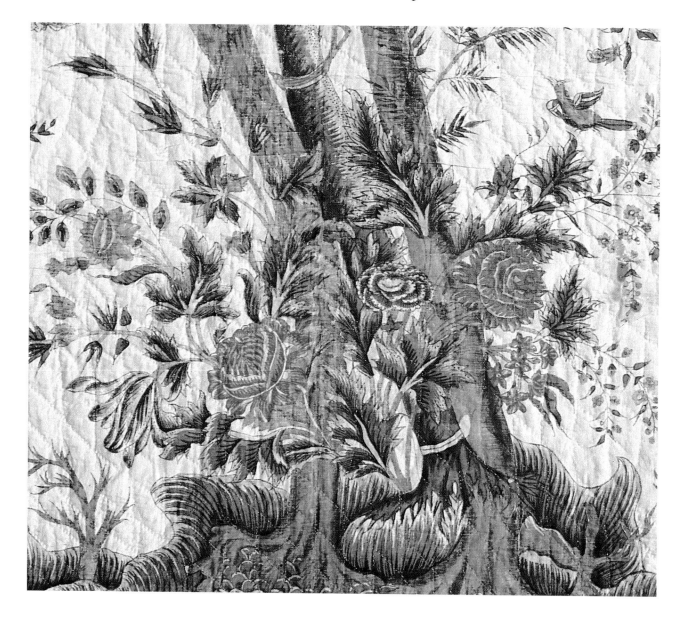

. . . This Quilt was purchased 1736 of a Smuggler of East India goods in the Isle of White, England. (Belonging to my late friend Miss Bradford.

Elizabeth Smith
Charleston

This inked inscription is written in the upper left corner of the Indian painted-and-dyed cotton palampore, or bed cover, which was used as the top of this quilt. It is under the quilting threads and refers only to the quilt top, which was probably lined and quilted in the mid-nineteenth century. The 1736 date for the palampore may be in error; its design is more typical of the latter half of the eighteenth century.

On the reverse of the inscribed corner is a crude stamp, probably an agent's mark in Tamil, the language of Madras on the South Coast of India where the palampore would have been made. According to the donor, the quilt had been given at one time to Thomas Sully by a woman whose portrait he painted, and he used it in a guest bedroom of the home in Philadelphia provided him by the philanthropist Stephen Girard.

Cotton top and lining. Cotton fiber filling.

CALIMANCO QUILT

Original quilt: wool top and lining, brown wool fiber filling.
Addition: cotton and wool lining, cotton fiber filling.

91 × 94 inches

This indigo-blue wool counterpane, or quilted bed cover, was made by Esther Wheat for her dower chest. A twin, she was born in 1774 in Conway, Massachusetts, and married Benjamin Lee in 1799. The shiny surface of the worsted fabric of the quilt top was achieved by calendering, a process of applying heat and pressure with metal plates or rollers. These glazed wools, or "calimancoes," were also frequently used in quilted petticoats.

According to Esther Lee's great-great-granddaughter, when the original plain-weave yellow wool lining of the quilt wore thin, Esther's daughter, Olive Lee Doolittle, added a second lining of red twill-weave cotton and wool. She added a thin layer of cotton fiber filling between the two linings, and quilted the added filling and lining to the original lining, but not through the quilt top.

REVERSE APPLIQUÉ QUILT

Cotton top; name and date embroidered in silk. Linen lining. Cotton fiber lining.   99 × 88 inches

In reverse appliqué, the positions of the pattern and background fabrics are reversed from those of onlaid appliqué. The silhouette of the pattern is cut out of the background fabric, and openings are filled by applying a contrasting fabric from underneath. Reverse appliqué was used less often in American quilts than onlaid.

This rare dated and signed example has a center panel and eight border motifs in reverse appliqué; the remainder of the quilt top is of simple geometric pieced work. The year "1795" and the name "M. Campbell" are embroidered in dark brown silk cross-stitches and eye-stitches along one side of the center panel.

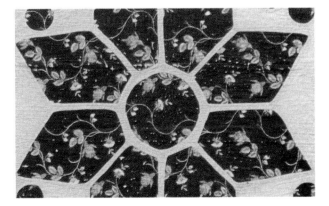

The top of this quilt is of cotton that was block printed and painted in England or France in the late eighteenth century. The fabric was probably originally used in bed furniture that might have included curtains at the sides, head, and foot that could enclose the whole bed, a bed cover, and valances around the top and base. When the ample bed furniture became worn or faded, there was frequently enough usable fabric to make entire quilts, like this one. This is a way in which larger pieces of fabric used in early America have been saved.

This printed cotton must have been popular in eighteenth-century America. A similar quilt in the collections of the DAR Museum in Washington, D.C., was made in about 1840 by Mary Sill of Old Lyme, Connecticut, from bed curtains that belonged to her mother, Mehitable Mather. The same fabric borders a quilt made probably before 1806 by Maria Lush of Albany, New York, which is now in the Denver Art Museum in Colorado. Another quilt in the national collection, dated 1802 and made by Mary Mitchell of Philadelphia, utilizes the printed design of the same fabric for an appliquéd flowering tree in the center.

This quilt came to the museum with only the information that it had a tenuous connection to the Washington family. Another quilt in which the printed fabric was used for seven appliquéd trees, is in Fredericksburg, Virginia, at Kenmore, the home of George Washington's sister, Bettie Washington Lewis. That quilt was said to have been worked successively by the three wives of Captain Thomas Hammond of Charles Town, Virginia, whose second wife was Mildred Washington, a niece of George Washington. It is tempting to speculate that there may be a connection between the fabrics in these two quilts. This quilt in its present form was made no earlier than the mid-nineteenth century since its lining, shown above, is a printed cotton of that period.

BLOCK-PRINTED COTTON QUILT

Cotton top. Printed cotton lining. Cotton fiber filling.

93 × 79 inches

— MARTHA WASHINGTON'S QUILT TOP —

Cotton.   104 × 104 inches

This Quilt was entirely the work of my Grandmother as far as the plain borders I finish'd it in 1815 & leave it to my Rosebud
E. P. Custis

The center of this quilt top was made by Martha Washington, a prolific needlewoman. The note, left, was written by her granddaughter, Eliza Parke Custis Law, a prolific note writer. The "Rosebud" to whom she addressed the note is her own daughter, Eliza L. Rogers.

A reproduction of one of the fabrics used in the pieced center appears in the Centennial Print Quilt on page 74.

1812 QUILT

Cotton top and lining. Cotton fiber filling.

90 × 82 inches

This quilt was donated to the museum in 1962 by the great-great-granddaughter of one of the quiltmakers, a Mrs. Adams. She and other family members are said to have made the quilt while the men were away during the War of 1812. The simple pieced pinwheel blocks alternate with plain white blocks of elaborate stuffed quilting in ten different designs, all but one repeated.

FRAMED CENTER QUILT

Most of the top is of all-cotton fabrics, with some all-linen, linen-and-cotton, and linen-and-silk fabrics. Linen lining. Cotton fiber filling.

84 × 81 inches
Lower corners are cut out

This example of pieced work is one of the first three quilts collected by the museum in the late nineteenth century. It was made by one or more members of a prosperous New England family—the Copps, of Stonington, Connecticut. The clothing and furnishing fabrics used in the quilt top span a period of about forty years. This, and the fact that the Copp family were in the dry goods business, may explain why the quilt includes more than one hundred and fifty different printed, woven-patterned, and plain fabrics of cotton, linen, and silk.

Although the array of fabrics is extravagant, economy is evident in the use of even the smallest scraps. Many blocks in the quilt pattern are composed of several smaller, irregularly shaped pieces. The lining is pieced of much-mended linen and cotton fabrics that were probably originally sheets. On one piece, the initials "HV" are cross-stitched in tan silk thread.

The arrangement of the pattern is one found frequently in eighteenth-century and early nineteenth-century quilts, a succession of borders framing a center panel of pieced work or appliqué. A view of the pieced center of this quilt seen from the right side, suggests the shape of a tree, and the printed fabrics repeat in mirror fashion in each row about 90 percent of the time. Perhaps the center was erroneously placed in this direction, or it was meant to be viewed from the bedside.

Two dresses in the Copp family collection are made of fabrics that appear in the quilt. One dress, right, dates from about 1800, and the other from about 1815, the time when the quilt was probably made.

CHILD'S QUILT

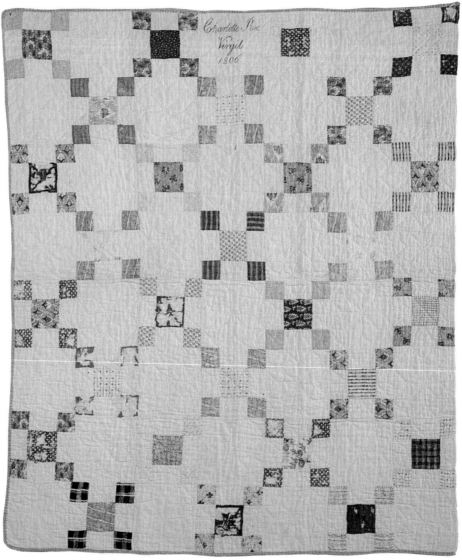

Cotton top with inscription embroidered in silk.
Cotton lining. Cotton fiber filling.

41 × 34 inches

In the spring of 1797 John E. Roe . . . came up the river and prepared a log cabin in Virgil. He . . . peeled bark for a roof and agreed with a man to put it on . . . then went down the Tioughnioga to get his wife, bringing her in a sleigh from Oxford. . . .

When they came to the river at a place called Messengerville, they saw Mr. Chaplin's house on the opposite bank. It was winter and the river was high, and the canoe that had been used in crossing was carried away. Mr. Chaplin's hog trough was secured, and Mrs. Roe was safely carried over on it . . . a whole day was consumed in negotiating the road over the hill to Virgil. . . . When they arrived they were surprised to find their house without a covering and the snow deep on the floor. . . .

In after years, Mrs. Roe enjoyed telling the story of her experience . . . and she always ended by saying, "And what do you think! The horses were so hungry that they ate the seats out of my nice rush-bottomed chairs."

STORIES OF CORTLAND COUNTY
by Bertha E. Blodgett, Cortland, New York, 1932

Charlotte and John Roe stayed on in Virgil to rear five children. This crib quilt is marked in brown silk backstitch, "Charlotte Roe Virgil 1806." It was probably made for their third child, John M., who was born in 1806.

DOUBLE IRISH CHAIN

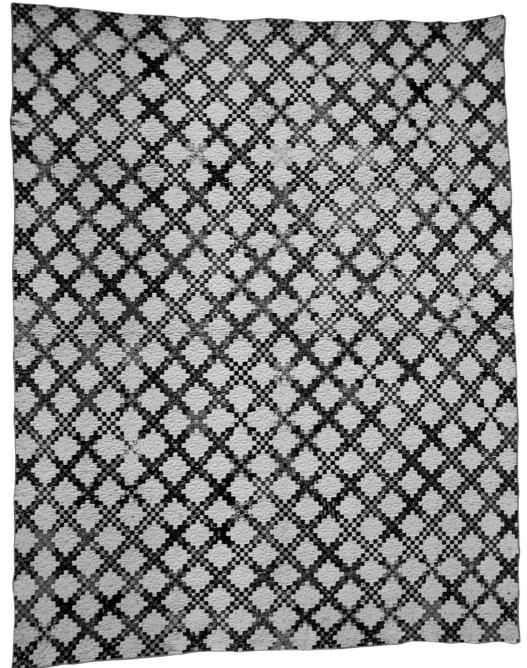

Cotton top and lining. Cotton fiber filling.

88 × 72 inches

Jane Valentine's quilt was donated to the National Museum in 1915 by one of her daughters, with the information that her mother started the quilt at the age of fourteen. Inscribed in ink on the front is "Commenced in 1825 & Finished in 1830 by Miss Jane Valentine Scipio Cayuga Co. N.Y. No. of Pieced Blocks 168." and "Small blocks 4,2,42." On the lining, the donor's sister wrote in a different hand, "My Mothers 5040 Blocks 1832 In Case of My death to be given to My Sister Hattie Blodgett." None of the inscribed counts appear to be correct; there are 348 white cruciform-shaped pieces, and 348 pieced blocks made of 10,092 squares, each 5/8 inch.

— BRITISH SAILOR'S BARTERED QUILT —

Wool. Wool embroidery.

95 × 81 inches

This early nineteenth-century pieced, appliquéd, and embroidered bed cover was made by sailors aboard a British vessel. It is made of napped woolen cloths, the red of which is said to have been cut from the uniforms of British soldiers who fought in the War of 1812. Exposed cut edges can be found in clothing of the period that are made of these sturdy wool fabrics. Here, the edges of the appliqué are not turned under and have not raveled.

The sailors gave their elaborate needlework in trade for money owed to a Mr. Graf, a tavernkeeper on the New York waterfront. The quilt descended in Mr. Graf's family to the present owner.

PRINTED QUILT CENTER

Cotton top and lining. Cotton fiber filling.

116 × 115 inches

The central diagonal block of this handsome quilt, specially printed to be used as a quilt center or cushion cover, was one of many produced in the first half of the nineteenth century. It dates from between 1815 and 1830, as do the rest of the printed fabrics in the quilt, which belonged to Mrs. William Alston. She lived at Fairfield, her husband's plantation on the Waccamaw River, near Georgetown and Charleston, South Carolina.

RISING SUN QUILT

Cotton top and lining. Initials embroidered in silk. Cotton fiber filling.

94 × 96 inches

First, after all my lawful debts are paid and discharged, I give and bequeath to Rachel Mary Drake, daughter of William Drake, deceased, my large spread called the Rising Sun.
Will of Mary "Betsy" Totten as quoted by Florence Peto in HISTORIC QUILTS, New York, 1939

As the repertoire of quilt patterns grew, a vocabulary of colorful and descriptive names came into use. A Laurel Leaf and an Album quilt are listed in the *Official Catalogue of the First National Fair for the Exhibition of American Manufacturers* held in the City of Washington in May 1846. Old Maid's Puzzle, Double Irish Chain, Joseph's Coat, Drunkard's Path, and Rocky Road to Kansas are some of the names included in a catalogue of quilt patterns copyrighted in 1898 by the Ladies' Art Company of St. Louis.

While the precise name of an individual's quilt pattern was seldom recorded, Betsy Totten left no doubt of the name she gave this spectacular quilt or of its importance to her.

Betsy was born in 1781 in Tottenville, Staten Island, New York, and died in Westfield, New York, at the age of eighty. She married twice, but late, and had no children. The "Rachel" to whom she left her quilt was her sister's granddaughter.

The Rising Sun pieced pattern in the center of Betsy's quilt is an eight-pointed star measuring 76 inches across, and containing 648 diamond-shaped pieces of printed cottons arranged concentrically by color. Appliquéd between the points of the star are elaborate vases of flowers and birds, combining floral glazed chintzes with some of the same fabrics used in the star. A matching floral vine runs around the four sides of the quilt between a swag-and-bow border on the inside, and a chain along the outer edge. The appliquéd flower stems, vine, swags, bows, and chain are only 3/32 inch wide.

The initials "BT" are embroidered in red silk cross-stitch next to one of the corner vases.

Cotton top; silk embroidery. Cotton lining. Cotton fiber filling.   87 × 75 inches

The most common form of appliqué used in American quilts is onlaid, with designs cut out of fabric and stitched onto the surface of a contrasting background fabric. The two fabrics of this quilt top, a printed cotton and a plain white cotton, are used alternately for the appliqué and the background.

Susan Strong, the quilter, was born in Frederick County, Maryland, in 1809, but moved to Ohio after her marriage in 1831 to William Bell of Richland County. She could have made her quilt in Maryland or Ohio. For the center motif, she chose an adaptation of the Great Seal of the United States, a design popular in various decorative arts from the time Congress adopted the seal in 1782. The shield and the details on the eagle's head are worked in chain and satin stitches in silk thread, originally rose but now tan.

FRANCES M. JOLLY'S QUILT TOP

Wool top with one small piece of cotton at outer edge.
Wool and silk braids, silk ribbon, silk embroidery.

105 × 102 inches

A number of elaborate mid-nineteenth-century quilts survive that utilize the beautiful silk and fine wool clothing fabrics of the first half of the century. This signed and dated example came from an African-American family. Little about the maker is known; her family is said to have lived in Massachusetts and moved to Pinehurst, North Carolina.

African-American studies have generated an interest in the needlework of African-American women that may aid the search for more information about Frances M. Jolly.

There was exhibited at the late Mechanical Fair held at Chicago, Ill., by Mr. C. Taylor, of that place, a quilt composed of 9,800 pieces of silk, each of which was about an inch square, and all sewed with exceeding beauty and neatness. Its chief charm, however, was the great skill evinced in the ingenious blending of colors, so as to produce a proper effect in the representation of various figures which ornamented it in every part. A brilliant sun shone in the centre, the moon and stars beamed out from one corner, while in another appeared a storm in the heavens, with lowering clouds and flashes of lightning.

Around the border were various designs illustrative of the season and of the rapid growth of our western country. At one place appeared a barren heath, with Indians and hunters roaming over it; next, a trading post, as the first entrance of civilization; next, a military station, with the glorious banner of our country streaming from the flagstaff; then a city, and steamboats and vessels gliding in and out of port.

"Great Quilt," *Scientific American,*
Volume 5, Number 12, December 8, 1849

By the second quarter of the nineteenth century, quilts were commonly exhibited at agricultural and manufacturing fairs, where they were seen not only by local residents but also by people who traveled from other areas. There were few published quilt patterns before the end of the century, so these exhibitions offered quilters an opportunity to obtain ideas from a source other than a personal exchange with friends and relatives.

The quilt mentioned in *Scientific American* may well have been this one made by Mary Willcox Taylor in Detroit, Michigan. Mary is said to have lived previously at Fort Dearborn, which she depicted in one corner of her quilt, overlooking a river and boats, one of which is a side-wheeler with the name "Hillman" on the wheel cover. Fort Dearborn was a military outpost which was established on the site of a trading post early in the nineteenth century. It was located on the banks of the Chicago River near Lake Michigan, now the heart of the city of Chicago.

The center of Mary's quilt presents the heavens in various aspects, from sunny to stormy, from moonlit to rainbow-arrayed. While no Indians are readily apparent, a pair of fashionably dressed hunters with a spotted dog decorate the landscape around the quilt border, along with a group of contented cows and a pair of birds flanking a bowl of fruit painted on velvet.

FORT DEARBORN QUILT

Top of silks, including velvet, with a small amount of cotton velvet; silk embroidery, including chenille; watercolor. Silk lining. Cotton fiber filling. Silk fringe.

87 × 79 inches, including fringe

BRIDE'S QUILT

Silk top, including velvet, lined with cotton muslin; cotton fiber padding under appliqué; silk embroidery. Silk lining. No filling.

94 × 104 inches, including fringe

This quilt was donated to the museum in 1933 by Mary Jane Moran's daughter who said that her mother had made it as a bride of eighteen in Baltimore, Maryland, using one thousand and one skeins of silk thread for the quilting.

On March 2, 1846, Mary Jane Green married John J. Moran, who had received his medical degree the year before from the University of Maryland. Dr. Moran was the twenty-five-year-old superintendent of Washington College Hospital in Baltimore when the dying Edgar Allan Poe was brought there for emergency treatment on Wednesday, October 3, 1849. Poe was transferred to a tower room near the Morans' living quarters. Mary helped nurse him and, in contrast to the work of her beautiful and delicate quilt, helped prepare a shroud for his burial.

LOG CABIN AND CIDER QUILT

Cotton, silk embroidery, inked inscription.   87 × 87 inches

This cotton quilt top was purchased at a county fair by Lena Cohen of Montgomery County, Maryland, and was donated to the museum by her granddaughter in 1942. The appliquéd designs of the blocks are similar to many found on Maryland quilts of the mid-nineteenth century. One block is signed in ink "Rebecca Diggs," who perhaps made that block or all of them.

A log cabin with a barrel marked "Hard Cider" in front of it appears on another block, commemorating William Henry Harrison's "log cabin and cider" presidential campaign of 1840. The symbols were originated by the opposition party, but Harrison turned the tables and utilized them to identify himself with the common man. He won the election only to die of pneumonia a month after his inauguration.

ANN'S QUILT

Cotton.   100 × 85 inches

"This quilt was made in 1840 by Ann, a colored slave girl 16 yrs. old who wove and spun and took care of all linen on the plantation of Capt. and Mrs. William Womack (Aunt Patsy and Uncle Billy) in Pittsylvania Co. Virginia. Grandma Adams made her home with Aunt Patsy after her mother's death and inherited her large estate," wrote Mrs. Womack's great-niece, Florence Adams Dubois. Grandma Adams was probably Martha "Patsy" Womack's sister, and the Gertrude Adams whose name is written in ink on the corner of the reverse side of the bed cover.

Little else is known of the quiltmaker, Ann, except that she was still in the Womack household years later when William Womack wrote in his will, dated November 1, 1849, ". . . to my beloved wife Martha Womack during her natural life the following Negro slaves to wit, Ann . . . "

Ann's "quilt" is probably a quilt top that remained unlined and unquilted, but was made into a lightweight bed cover by finishing the edges.

Cotton top and lining. Cotton fiber filling.   80 × 81 inches

Mourning designs appear in many nineteenth-century decorative arts, including those of the needle. Embroidered landscapes, like the one shown right, usually worked by schoolgirls, show relatives or friends sorrowing before a monument dedicated to a lost loved one. Nancy Ward Butler, of Jamestown, New York, commemorated the death of her son's infant daughter in a quilt, with an appliquéd inscription reminiscent of the lettering on a tombstone: "NANCY · A · BUTLER · DIED · FEB · 3 *1842* AGED 20 mo."

The quilt was donated to the museum in 1976 by Nancy Ward Butler's great-great-granddaughter, and the namesake of the infant, Nancy A. Butler. With the quilt, carefully hand-lettered on paper, was an undated award, "Second Prize for the most Beautiful Quilt."

MASONIC SYMBOLS QUILT

Wool and silk top; embroidery in crinkled silk thread that may be untwisted silk twist. Cotton lining. Cotton fiber filling.

75 × 73 inches

The quilt above, embroidered with Masonic symbols, was made in about 1840 by Eliza Rosenkrantz Hussey whose husband, Edward, was a Mason and an Odd Fellow. Eliza was born in Pennsylvania in 1816, and married Edward in 1835. They first lived in Carlisle, Indiana, where their ten children were born. In various Indiana records, Edward is said to have sold Goods in Carlisle, to have operated the Na-

ODD FELLOWS QUILT

Silk top; embroidery in silk twist. Cotton lining. Cotton fiber filling.

84 × 85 inches

tional Hotel in Terre Haute, and to have been a bookkeeper and the postmaster in Brazil. In the 1860 census, Eliza is listed as a milliner.

In about 1845, Eliza made the quilt shown above, this one embroidered with such Odd Fellows symbols and inscriptions as "Educate the Orphan," "Be Temperate," "Remember the Widow," and "Bury the Dead."

ONE-PATCH PATTERN

Cotton top and lining. Cotton fiber filling in border only.

104 × 102 inches, including fringe

Patchwork may be made in various forms, as stars, triangles, diamonds, waves, stripes, squares, &c. The outside border should be four long strips of calico, all of the same sort and not cut into patches. The dark and light calico should always be properly contrasted in arranging patch-work.

Perhaps there is no patch-work that is prettier or more ingenious than the hexagon, or six-sided; this is also called honey-comb patch-work.

Godey's Lady's Book, Philadelphia, January 1835

Godey's Lady's Book continues with instructions for making hexagon patchwork "properly." It advises that, before stitching the hexagons of calico and white muslin together, each piece be basted over hexagons of stiff paper cut from old copy books or letters, leaving the papers in "to keep the patches in shape till the whole is completed."

Laura R. Dwight of Orangeburg, South Carolina, may well have used these instructions for her quilt. Her hexagons, about 17,871 of them, measure only ⅝ inch at their widest. The papers over which they must have been sewn to keep the points so precise and the piecing flat, have been removed as recommended.

Laura's quilt also conforms to the suggestions to "Let each ring consist of the same sort of calico, or at least of the same colour. . . . Put a border all round, of handsome calico, all of the same sort," and "In quilting . . . to follow the shape of the hexagons."

One-patch patterns, made of pieces of one size and shape, could be varied by the colors and placement of the fabrics.

Cotton top and lining. Cotton fiber filling.   91 × 86 inches

The gay belles of fashion may boast of excelling
  In waltz or cotillion—at whist or quadrille;
And seek admiration by vauntingly telling
  Of drawing and painting, and musical skill;
But give me the fair one in country and city,
  Whose home and its duties are dear to her heart,
Who cheerfully warbles some rustical ditty,
  While plying the needle—the swift flying needle,
The needle directed by beauty and art. . . .
        "The Needle," *Godey's Lady's Book,*
              Philadelphia, 1830

The museum's collections contain several products of the needle plied by Rachel Burr Corwin: three pieced-work quilts and two "comforts," as well as her spinning wheel, initialed "RC," and sheets and pillowcases for which she is said to have spun the linen.

Rachel was born in 1788, the daughter of Samuel and Sybil Burr of Massachusetts. On October 14, 1809, she married Samuel Corwin of Middle Hope, Orange County, New York. She died forty years later in Orange County. Late in life she made this quilt, choosing two multiple-patch patterns, Feathered Star and Garden Maze. While multiple-patch pieced work entails joining pieces of different shapes and sizes, it offers greater pattern variety than one-patch work.

VANITY OF VANITIES QUILT

Cotton top and lining. Cotton fiber filling.   85 × 102 inches

Toward the middle of the nineteenth century, the religious, moralistic, and mournful concerns recorded earlier by schoolgirls on samplers and embroidered pictures began to appear on quilts. In 1847, at the age of twenty-six, Emily Holbert may have drawn on her school experience to inscribe her quilt in bold appliqué.

INDUSTRY, AND PROPER IMPROVEMENT
OF TIME. VANITY OF VANITIES,
ALL IS VANITY. EMILY HOLBERT'S QUILT;
WORKED JANUARY, A.D. 1847.
CHESTER, ORANGE COUNTY, NEW YORK.
             Inscription around quilt border

Cotton top and lining. Cotton fiber lining and stuffing.   89 × 87 inches

The crossed flowers of the appliquéd blocks of this finely worked quilt are used in profile on the border's flowering vine. The signature block was made to stand out from the rest of the elaborate quilting by executing the name "Jane Barr" and the date "July 1849" in stuffed work.

The quilt was donated to the National Museum in 1954 by Jane Barr's niece.

QUAKER ALBUM QUILT

Cotton top, inked inscriptions. Cotton lining. Cotton fiber filling.   99 × 98 inches

This quilt was made for Hannah Nicholson by members of the Religious Society of Friends, or Quakers, who lived in and near Philadelphia. Hannah was born and lived in Indiana, but her father was from New Jersey, and it is the names of paternal aunts, uncles, and cousins that appear on the quilt. Hannah married another Indiana native, Howard Grave, whose family was among the earliest settlers in the state.

The quilt's inscriptions indicate that several blocks were made by women to be given in the names of male relatives or young children. Most of the blocks were made by Philadelphians, but six bear the names of New Jersey towns—Woodbury, Bordentown, Pleasant Hill, and Salem. Where dates appear, they are in the Quaker style: "3rd month 22nd 1843."

MALTAVILLE ALBUM QUILT

Cotton top with a small amount of silk in the appliqué of one block; silk and cotton embroidery. Cotton lining. Cotton fiber filling.

92 × 91 inches

You know, 'tis a rule for each individiwal that gives a square, to write her name on the middle on't, and if she's a mind to, a line or two of somethin'—say for instance, a varse—besides the name. Tildy Brockle called it a motter, and said she should write under her name—

"When the rose is red and the grass is green, The time will come that I have seen."

It sounded terrible shaller for to put on a square for a minister's wife, I thought, but then I didn't tell her so.

"Sketches from Real Life. Letter VIII—The Album Quilt, Etc."
Godey's Lady's Book, Philadelphia, August 1848

Album quilts were very popular in the middle of the nineteenth century. Like the pages of an autograph book, each quilt square bore the name or initials of the person who made or presented it. Album quilts were made to commemorate special occasions— a gift to a new bride or groom, a remembrance for a friend who was moving away, or a token to honor a highly regarded member of the community.

Sometimes the recipient started the quilt. As Florence Hartley relates in *The Ladies' Hand Book of Fancy and Ornamental Work*, written in 1859, "An Album quilt is a very pretty idea. A lady gives the size of the square she wishes to each of her lady friends, who are willing to contribute to her quilt. They make a square according to their own taste, putting a white piece in the centre, on which they write their name. Every lady's autograph adorns her own square."

The squares of this album quilt were made, joined, lined, and quilted in 1847 by the women of the Presbyterian Church of Maltaville, New York, for the wife of the pastor, the Reverend William Hill. The large center square contains a dedicatory poem with the inscription, "Presented to Mrs. Mary B. Hill as an expression of esteem by the ladies of Maltaville."

GROOM'S QUILT

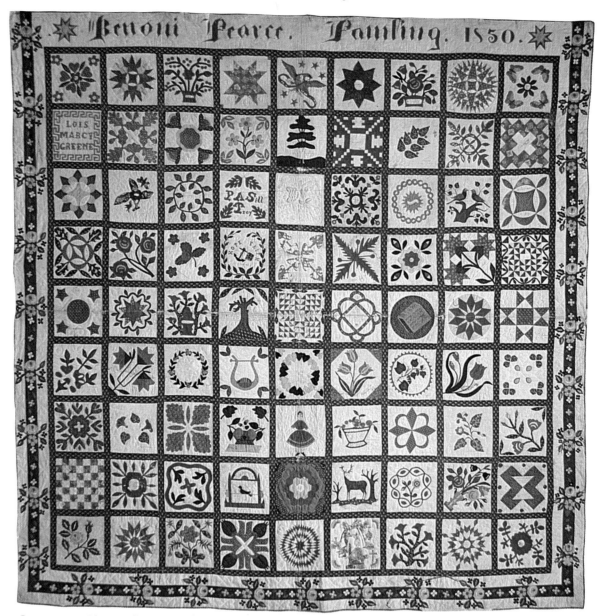

Cotton top, with a small amount of silk in the appliqué; details and inscriptions in ink and silk and cotton embroidery. Cotton lining. Cotton fiber filling.

104 × 103 inches

This quilt was made for Benoni Pearce in 1850 when he was twenty-eight years old. The eighty-one squares are signed by friends and members of his family, including his mother, Lucretia, his thirty-year-old sister, Lydia, and at least two cousins and two aunts. Benoni was then a farmer living on his father's farm in Pawling, Duchess County, New York. By 1860, census records show that Benoni was still farming with his father, but he had acquired a wife, Emma, and two children, seven-year-old Augusta and three-year-old Jesse.

In 1972, Benoni's quilt was donated to the Smithsonian by his granddaughter and great-granddaughter, with the information that it was presented to him for his betrothal.

SEAMSTRESSES' QUILT

Cotton top and lining. Cotton fiber filling.   92 × 93 inches

This quilt was made in the middle of the nineteenth century in the Baltimore County home of George Slothower. He was a wholesale dry goods merchant and the owner of two cotton mills, the Powhatan and Pocahontas Mills. He also had an interest in the Phoenix Mill.

The quilt was donated to the museum by George and Emily Slothower's great-granddaughter who explained that the family had retained two resident seamstresses, usually with German or Dutch names, who made the family clothing, and it was probably they who made the quilt.

But the Sewing Machine is an American invention. Machinery is the grand necessity of the United States, for population has not augmented to a point which renders the number of needlewomen adequate to the demand upon their industry. America almost denudes Germany of her Sempstresses, and still production falls short of her requirements. She is thus compelled to employ Steel and Iron to do the work of humanity. . . .

"On Stitching Machines,"
Journal of the Society of Arts,
London, January 20, 1854

49

ELIZA BAILE'S BRIDE'S QUILT

Cotton top; details and inscriptions in ink and watercolor; silk, cotton, and wool embroidery; paper templates under some appliqué. Cotton lining. Cotton fiber filling.

93 × 93 inches

What little girl does not recollect her first piece of patchwork, the anxiety for fear the pieces would not fit, the eager care with which each stitch was taken, and the delight of finding the bright squares successfully blended into the pretty pattern. Another square and another, and the work begins to look as if in time it might become a quilt; then, as the little girl grows up to young ladyhood, the blushes flit across her cheeks when, as she bends over her sewing, grandmamma suggests that making patchwork is a sign of matrimonial anticipations. . . .

THE LADIES' HAND BOOK
OF FANCY AND ORNAMENTAL WORK,
by Miss Florence Hartley, Philadelphia, 1859

If the quilt Eliza Jane Baile made in anticipation of matrimony is an indication, she must have practiced her patchwork as a little girl with "eager care" and much success.

Eliza was born in 1832 in Carroll County, Maryland, an area in which many beautiful quilts were made in the mid-nineteenth century. Eliza's quilt was no exception, with its twenty-five squares of beautifully worked, richly colored flowers and fruit surrounded by a continuous vine bearing bas relief strawberries. Near the top, a scroll nestling in morning glories contains appropriately sentimental lines of poetry:

> *Sweett flowers bright as Indian Sky*
> *Yet mild as Beauty's soft blue eye;*
> *Thy charms tho' unassuming shed*
> *A modest splendoure o'er the mead.*

On another scroll, in one corner of the quilt, Eliza recorded her name and the date she began the work, "E. J. Baile commence'd June 1850." When Eliza married Levi Manahan on October 11th, she didn't quite have her quilt finished. In the opposite corner there is a scroll with the inscription, "Finished October 30 1851."

SUNBURST QUILT

Cotton top and lining. Cotton fiber filling and stuffing.

98 × 89 inches

This quilt was made in the mid-nineteenth century, in Funkstown, Maryland, by Anna Sophie Shriver for her sister, Catherine Shriver Knode, wife of Frisbe Knode. It is exquisitely worked, with a pieced sunburst pattern complemented by elaborate stuffed quilting.

The quilt was inherited by Catherine and Frisbe's son, William Shriver Knode, who passed it on to his daughter. She in turn requested that upon her death it be given to a museum for safekeeping. When she died, in 1940, her husband, William F. Heft, gave it to the National Museum in her name.

Cotton top; embroidery mostly cotton with some silk; cotton fiber stuffing in some of the appliquéd motifs; inscriptions in ink and cotton and silk embroidery. Cotton lining. Cotton fiber filling.

107 × 107 inches

This album quilt was probably made about 1860, perhaps for a member of the Wilmer family of Kent County, Maryland. Much of its elaborate appliqué was made three-dimensional by gathering folded strips of fabric and stitching them down in various shapes, while some of the motifs are padded with cotton fibers under the appliqué. Twelve of the twenty-five blocks have embroidered, inked, or stamped signatures or initials.

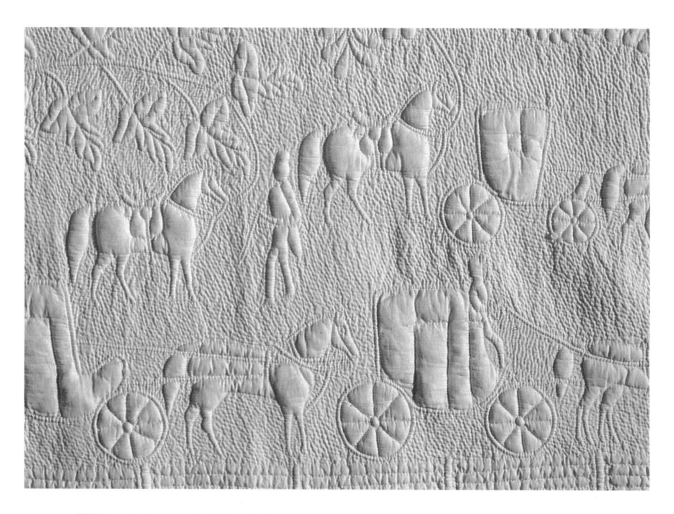

This outstanding example of stuffed quilting was made by Virginia M. Ivey, left, daughter of Mourning Mason and David Anderson Ivey. Although born in Tennessee, Virginia was named for her father's native state. From Tennessee, David Ivey moved his family to Logan County, Kentucky, where Virginia, who never married, lived in his home until he died. She divided her remaining years between the homes of her sister, who lived in Kentucky, a brother of New Orleans, Louisiana, and another brother of Little York, Illinois.

Virginia, or Jennie as she was called by her family, got the inspiration for her quilt from the bustling activity of a mid-nineteenth-century Kentucky fair. Fairgrounds were usually located on a beautiful and easily accessible site just outside a town that could accommodate the influx of visitors from far and near; thus Jennie identifies her needlework: "1856 A REPRESENTATION OF THE FAIR NEAR RUSSELLVILLE KENTUCKY." This block-lettered legend is worked in tiny quilting stitches just inside a paling fence that surrounds the quilt's center.

Within the fence, horses, carriages, cattle, sheep, and chickens circle a judges' stand. Another paling fence, with gates in the center of two sides, serves as the quilt's outer border, and encloses the rest of the fairground. There people visit exhibit buildings; or congregate, stroll, and ride in carriages or on horseback around the tree-lined perimeter.

RUSSELLVILLE FAIR

Cotton top and lining. Cotton fiber filling and stuffing.   95 × 98 inches, including fringe

LITTLE SISTER'S QUILT

Cotton top. Name stencilled in ink on cotton lining. Cotton fiber filling.   92 × 95 inches

Stencilled in the center of the lining of this quilt is the name "S. T. Holbert." It belonged to Susan Theresa Holbert of Chester, New York. She was born in 1834 and married William Alfred Lawrence in 1861. The quilt was probably made a few years before her marriage.

Susan's sister, Emily Holbert Finch, who was fourteen years older, died in 1858. She made the inscription quilt on page 43 in 1847. Perhaps Emily made this quilt for Susan, or they both had a talent for skilled needlework and Susan made this quilt herself.

Cotton top and lining. Cotton fiber filling.   86 × 87 inches

Mary Rockhold-Teter of Noblesville, Indiana, made this quilt during the Civil War, when patriotic symbols were much on the minds of Americans. The design, adapted from the American flag and named Stars and Stripes, appeared in the July 1861 issue of *Peterson's Magazine*, a women's periodical published in Philadelphia.

Thirty-four stars are appliquéd in the center, representing the number of states in the Union from July 4, 1861, until July 4, 1863. The same number of stars are appliquéd around the border.

Mary made the quilt for her son, George, a Union soldier. In the quilting she included his name, the names of Generals Scott and Taylor under whom he served, "Genral Lyon," the president of the United States as "Abe" and "Ab Lyncoln," the word "Cat," and the year, 1861. Written in ink on the lining is "Geoge Teter."

She was of a family of strong, patriotic Revolutionary stock, and inherited a willingness to do and to labor that the country might grow. Her grand-father was Capt. John Rockhold, a native of Pennsylvania, who served in the War for Independence. Her father, Joseph Rockhold, moved from Pennsylvania to Ohio in 1800. He was a captain in the War of 1812. This trait of patriotism was one of the strongest in the character of Mrs. Teter. During the late war she showed her great love for the soldier boys in many ways, aiding in every way she could to encourage and help in the country's peril.

Obituary of Mary Rockhold-Teter, 1897

This quilt was made in Nashville Tenn. I began just before the Civil War, the day Tenn seceded I stitched the U.S. Flag in the center of the quilt, my Father being a loyal man he had to leave home or be forced in the Confederate service, I carried the quilt through the rebel lines to the federal to Cincinnati we remained in Cincinnati until the fall of Fort Donelson then we returned home to Nashville. After the battle of Stone River Gen'l Rosecrans suggested I make an autograph quilt of it & at his headquaters (sic) his was the first name placed in the flag and the second was James A. Garfield and most of his Staff Officers names were placed around the flag. Gen'l Winfield Scott in 1863 at West Point wrote his name. I was visiting my Brother who was a Cadet at the Point. Then Abraham Lincoln 1863 his Son Robert Lincoln in 1881. P. H. Sheridan U.S. Grant Brig Gen'l L. Thomas Adjt Gen'l U.S.A. Maj Gen'l George H. Thomas Benj F Butler Chester A. Arthur. S. H Wilson. Gen H. W. Blair W. T. Serman J. St. Clair Morton. Jas McLear Horace Maynard. Col Bowman Supt West Point 1863. Jas S Negley. A McDowell McCook J. A. Garfield Chief of Staff. Jas McKibben. Col Arthur Ducat. C. G. Harker. W. W. Averill Wm McKinley. Nelson N Miles. Leland Stanford. Theodore Roosevelt. Sen Jos R. Hawley. This quilt was saluted by 20000 troops at the funeral of Pres Lincoln. hung over the East door of the rotunda when Pres Garfield's body lay in State, has been hung out at different Inaugurations. It has the line of Gen'ls & Lt Gen'ls. It has other names but these are the most prominent. The different ones that have had charge of it when on exhibition have not been very careful with it. I have never thought of disposing of it, but having lost my home through fire, I wish to rebuld (sic) & this is the only way I can see to raise money. Mary A. Lord.

Mary Hughes Lord's undated description of her own quilt

Among the "prominent" signatures on Mary's quilt is that of James Morton, who gave her the album in which she kept her photograph as well as those of family and friends, many of them Civil War soldiers. James was killed at the battle of Petersburg, Virginia, on June 17, 1864, but Mary saved his letters and official service documents.

Born in Nashville in 1848, Mary was seventeen years old when she married Henry Edward Lord, who had served in Tennessee in the Indiana Volunteers. They lived in his home in Brooklyn, New York, and later in the Washington, D.C. area. Mary died in Baltimore, Maryland, in 1926. Her quilt was never sold, but instead passed to her daughter, who brought it to the National Museum in 1943.

Silk top; embroidered details, inked inscriptions. Silk lining. Cotton fiber filling

72 × 83 inches

RAISED APPLIQUÉ QUILT

Cotton top and lining. Cotton fiber stuffing and perhaps a thin layer of filling.   89 × 92 inches

Mary Palmer

Deborah Palmer

The stuffed work of the central fruit basket and grape wreaths of this ornate quilt are complemented by the three-dimensional effect of the padded appliqué. Cotton fibers have been inserted under all the red and green appliquéd fabrics used for the rose wreath and basket design, except for the stems, which are green cotton fabric wrapped around rolls of white cotton fabric.

Although raised appliqué was often used for details in mid-nineteenth-century American quilts, it is unusual to find such an elaborate design treated this way in its entirety.

The quilt was so meticulously designed by Mary Palmer that the arrangement of the flowers in each corner basket is a mirror image of the arrangement in the next corner around the quilt. Born in 1830 and a lifelong resident of Otsego County, New York, Mary made the quilt with the help of her sister, Deborah.

FRUIT AND FLOWERS QUILT

Cotton top and lining. Cotton fiber filling and stuffing.

89 × 89 inches

Quiltmaking filled a special need in the life of Mary Carpenter Pickering of St. Clairsville, Ohio, who is said to have started this quilt in about 1850 to make the time go more quickly when her friend, John Bruce Bell, joined a wagon train for the Oregon Territory. After his return, they married on September 3, 1861. Then John joined the Union Army for service in the Civil War. During his absence, Mary made another quilt, which is treasured by her grandson's family.

GARDEN OF EDEN QUILT

Cotton top with some of the appliqué in silk; cotton and silk embroidery.   86 × 75 inches
Cotton lining. Cotton fiber filling and stuffing; the fruit on one of the trees
has a layer of heavy paper between the silk appliqué and the stuffing.

In the center of this quilt there is a representation of the firmament with the sun,
stars, and four phases of the moon. Around the border are Old Testament vignettes
depicting the Garden of Eden, Eve being tempted by the serpent, Eve giving Adam
the apple, and Adam and Eve running out of the Garden of Eden.

In about 1900, Laura Doty Diffey purchased this quilt at a church bazaar in Fort
Smith, Arkansas. It is almost certainly the work of Sylvia S. Queen of Olathe, Kan-
sas, whose quilt with similar vignettes is in the collection of the Johnson County
Museum of Shawnee, Kansas.

MACHINE QUILTING

Cotton top, backing, and lining. Cotton fiber and cord stuffing.

76 × 63 inches

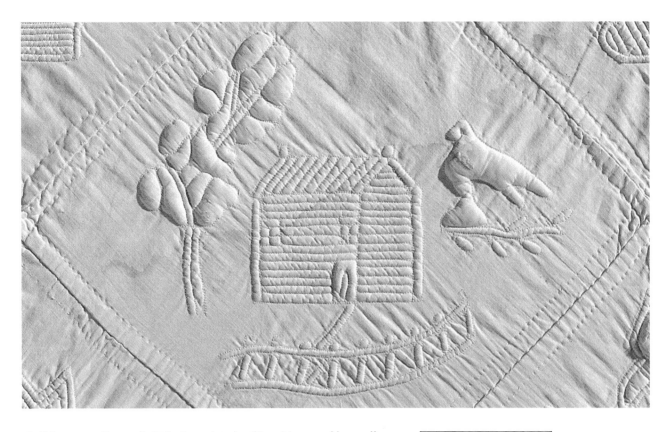

Quilting on a Grover & Baker's sewing machine, is no trouble at all, and the rapidity with which it is accomplished, enables us to apply it to many things which would cost too much time and labor for hand sewing.

THE LADIES' HAND BOOK OF
FANCY ORNAMENTAL WORK by Miss Florence Hartley,
Philadelphia, 1859

The invention of the double-thread chain stitch is attributed to William Grover. In 1851, he and William Baker received a patent for a machine that sewed with this stitch. While most elaborate quilting of the nineteenth century was done by hand, the unknown maker of this quilt used just such a machine to stitch the design of each square through two layers of cotton fabric. The design areas were then stuffed with cotton fibers. The squares were sewn together by hand to make the quilt top, an overall lining was added, and the three layers were quilted by hand along each side of the seams where the squares of the quilt top were joined.

In the 1860s, the Grover and Baker double-thread chain-stitch machine succumbed to competition from lockstitch machines that used one-third the amount of thread and made less bulky seams. The lockstitch remains the standard stitch of home sewing machines to this day.

The motifs of this all-white quilt are similar to those found on many of the colorful appliqué quilts of the mid-nineteenth century. The quilt's design and the use of the Grover and Baker stitch suggest that this is an early example of machine quilting, although more elaborate than most of the work for which the new machines were used—simple designs for linings and utilitarian clothing.

This quilt was made in Brooklyn, New York, by Susan Rogers. It consists of twenty-five blocks, each with a different design and most with the embroidered name or initials of a family member. There are blocks symbolizing military service or membership in benevolent and fraternal organizations. A basket of flowers has embroidered under it the name "Nettie," Susan's daughter who was about thirteen years old when the quilt was made. The initials "E L" are embroidered in the center of a floral-geometric design, probably for Emma Louise, Susan's ten-year-old daughter.

A vase decorated with the image of a young boy, cut from a printed cotton, and filled with flowers, has "Mother" embroidered underneath it. The design of the center block is a tree decorated with baskets of fruit and flowers, oranges, stockings, a cane, a candy cane, a ladder, parasols, an umbrella, a bottle of bitters, a fish, a bird, a mitten, a slipper, a picture of a dog in an oval frame, a cat on a mat, a pipe, a watch, a bird in a cage, and other gifts; a few marked with names or initials. Under the fenced-in base of the tree, Susan embroidered "Merry Christmas."

At the lower left corner of the quilt is a tree filled with birds. On one branch there is a robin holding a worm in its beak, and a nest with three open-mouthed baby birds begging to be fed, while a seated cat waits patiently below. Beneath this design Susan Rogers embroidered her name and the date, 1867. The quilt was donated to the museum by the wife of Susan Rogers's great-great-grandson.

Cotton top; silk and cotton embroidery. Cotton lining. Cotton fiber filling.   83 × 85 inches

SOLAR SYSTEM QUILT

Wool top; wool braid; wool and silk embroidery. Cotton and wool lining. Cotton fiber filling.   89 × 106 inches

Sarah Ellen Harding, who was born in Cincinnati, Ohio, in 1847, married Marion Baker of Cedar County, Iowa, on October 10, 1867. They lived in Cedar County until 1878, then moved to Johnson County where he had a general merchandise business in Lone Tree. Ellen Harding Baker, left, had seven children before she died of tuberculosis in the spring of 1886.

In 1983, Ellen's striking and unusual quilt was donated to the National Museum by two of her granddaughters, one of whom observed, "The design, which is not a traditional one, bears some resemblance to solar systems illustrated in astronomy books of the time. The quilt was used by Mrs. Baker as a visual aid for lectures she gave on astronomy in the towns of West Branch, Moscow, and Lone Tree, Iowa."

FAMILY VIGNETTE

Cotton. Embroidery in silk and cotton.   100 × 80 inches

Josiah Hasbrouck of Ulster County, New York, was born in 1830 and married Ellen Jane Blauvelt in 1856, just before her seventeenth birthday. They had five sons, but the first, Gilbert, born in 1856, died in infancy. The youngest was born in 1864.

This charming counterpane was said to have been made by an Englishwoman for the Hasbroucks, who may be the man and woman under the tree and the four boys in rowboats below, their sons. The 1870 census report lists Josiah as a physician, his wife, Ellen, as keeping house, and their four sons—Walter, another son named Gilbert, John, and Josiah. Also listed as part of the household is a domestic servant, twenty-four-year-old Mary Ward who was born in Ireland. Perhaps Mary, or someone else who worked in the household, made the counterpane.

CHESTNUT BURR TABLE COVER

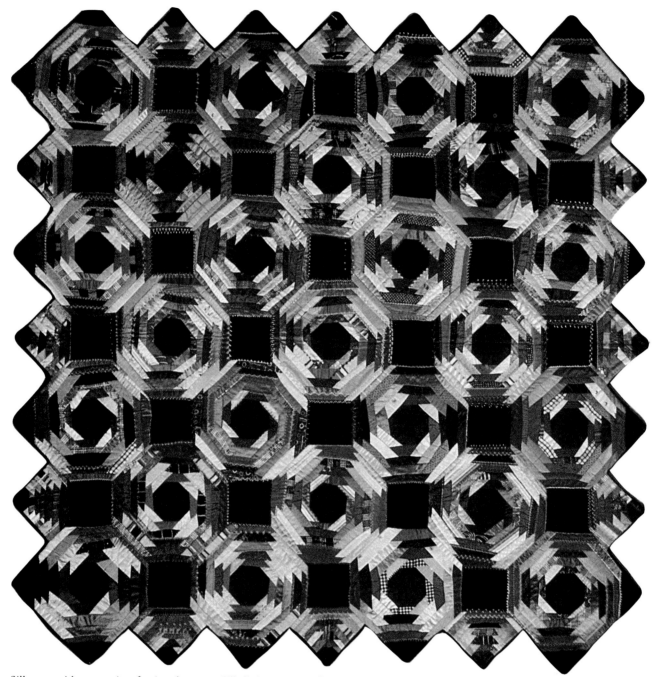

Silk top, with one strip of printed cotton. Silk lining. Cotton fiber filling between pieces and templates.   64 × 64 inches

. . . *Patchwork can be used for a variety of things, such as sofa pillows, chair cushions, table covers, tidies, etc.*
. . . *The log cabin design, familiar to all readers, is very pretty.*
FANCY WORK RECREATIONS by Eva Marie Niles,
Minneapolis, Minnesota, 1885

This table cover was made in about 1860 in Earlville, Illinois, by the grandmother of the donor. The pieced pattern she chose is called Chestnut Burr and is a variation of a Log Cabin design.

Top of silk pieced work and silk-chenille embroidery has a cotton lining and cotton fiber filling. Red silk underside has a printed cotton lining and cotton fiber filling.

74 × 65 inches

Using an elaborate throw in the parlor gave the needlewoman an opportunity to show off her work. The unknown woman who made this beautiful throw in the latter half of the nineteenth century complemented intricate hexagon and diamond pieced work with a center and border of black velvet embroidered with rose designs in silk chenille, a pile-surfaced yarn. Even the lining of her tour de force was lovely—a second quilt of fine red silk impressively quilted with red silk thread.

Silk and Velvet Sofa Quilt.—A most useful, and in these days of draperies, an ornamental adjunct as well, to a sofa, is a silk quilt. It is substituted for tidies.
BLAKELEE'S INDUSTRIAL CYCLOPEDIA,
by George E. Blakelee, New York, 1889

OCEAN WAVE QUILT

Cotton top and lining. Cotton fiber filling.   83 × 76 inches

Mary Ann Bishop, who was born in 1819 and died in 1915, lived in Wilkesville, Vinton County, Ohio. In 1936, her daughter donated to the museum two pieced-work quilts made by her, one in an Ocean Wave pattern and the other in a Double Nine-Patch. Both quilts have a sawtooth border pattern and a distinctive S-curved motif in the quilting pattern. Two wooden templates, left, used for marking this

DOUBLE NINE-PATCH QUILT

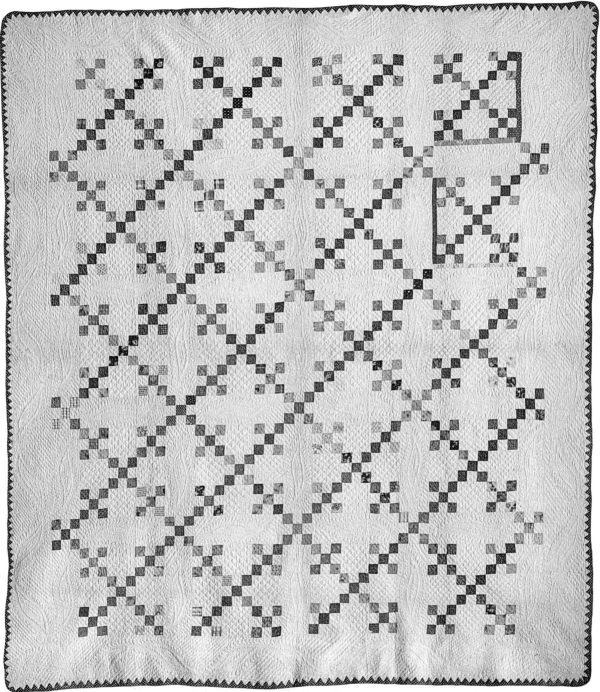

Cotton top and lining. Cotton fiber filling.

95 × 85 inches

part of the quilting pattern were donated with the quilts. Traces of the marks on the Ocean Wave quilt seem to be in pencil. On the Double Nine-Patch quilt, the marks were made in pencil or charcoal.

Two of the blocks of the Double Nine-Patch quilt were smaller than the rest, and were enlarged by adding strips of printed cotton along two edges.

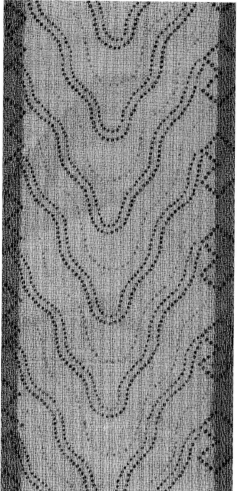

Many cottons printed with commemorative designs were manufactured when the United States celebrated its first hundred years of independence. This quilt is composed of centennial fabric samples sent by manufacturers to John Bradbury, a dry goods merchant in New York City. It was made in Charlestown, New Hampshire, by Bradbury's wife, Emily, their twelve-year-old daughter, Harriet, and Emily's mother, Maria Silsby Robertson.

The pattern of each fabric is obviously patriotic, except for a striped design in various colors. It was copied from the fabric of a favorite gown of Martha Washington, the bodice of which is still at Mount Vernon, her home in Virginia. The skirt was reused in a dress by her granddaughter, Eliza Parke Custis Law. In 1820, Eliza used the skirt fabric a second time to make "sweet bags," small drawstring bags for holding aromatic mixtures, to sell at a charity fair.

Martha Washington used pieces of her gown fabric in her quilt top, shown on page 20.

CENTENNIAL-PRINT COTTON QUILT

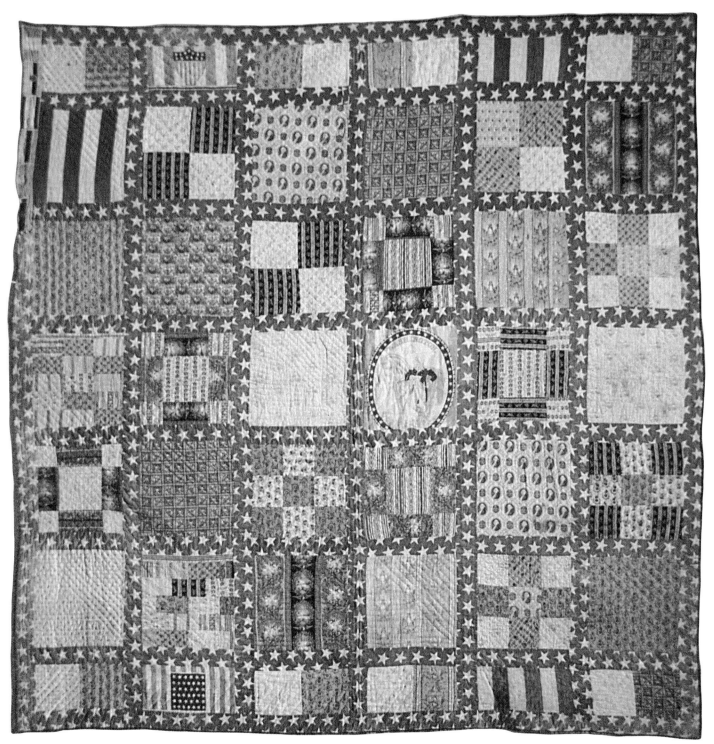

Cotton top and lining. Cotton fiber filling.   80 × 81 inches

NURSE'S QUILT

Cotton.   87 × 86 inches

Betty West, our Negro nurse, made this quilt for my brother Kennedy and me. The many stitches made by stiff old fingers showes the real love she had for the two white children entrusted to her care. I treasured the quilt & have kept it all these years in loving memory of her.
Mary C. Watkins, Oct. 24, 1939

This quilt top was made in about 1879 by Betty West who was employed by Leonides C. Campbell and his wife, Mary, as a nurse for their children, John Clement Kennedy Campbell and Mary Campbell. John (or Kennedy) was born in 1870 and was four years older than Mary, who wrote the note. She is the mother of Kennedy C. Watkins who, with his wife, donated the quilt top to the museum in 1975.

Silk top; silk embroidery, including chenille; gold and silver metallic embroidery; spangles and pearls. Lining of heavy pattern-woven cotton and silk. No filling.

111 × 105 inches

This large, heavy bed cover consists of fifty-six embroidered, painted, and crazy-patched blocks edged with 1/4-inch silver metallic braid, and a 9-inch red plush border edged with twisted red and gold silk cord.

Three of the blocks are dated 1883 and 1884, and the designs of all but four represent states and territories of the United States. The crazy patchwork block in the upper left is initialled "AH"; the third block from the left in the top row includes the British Royal Arms printed on silk; the right-hand block in the seventh row is embroidery on patterned silk; and the lower right-hand block is inscribed "the friend of all his race" and "God Bless him." In the center of the lining are the initials "WWC" embroidered with dark red silk over padding, with the outlines couched in gold thread.

The cover was made for William W. Corcoran (1799-1899), the founder of the Corcoran Gallery of Art in Washington, D.C. After his death, it hung in the Louise Home (for elderly women), which he also established.

To the maker and her friends it appeared a monumental labor of taste, industry, and artistic talent. To us it stood for a misdirected energy and perseverance too common among women . . . busy idleness has been made to seem improving . . . the makers of "crazy patchwork" seem to have eaten of the insane root that takes the reason prisoner.

Editorial, *Harper's Bazaar*
New York, September 13, 1884

Perhaps nothing is more typical of the Victorian era than elaborately decorated parlor throws and bed covers made of bits of silk and velvet. Although they were referred to as "crazy quilts," most were not quilted, but were tied or tacked intermittently. Packages of fabric samples could be purchased to make crazy quilts, as well as diagrams for assembling the pieces. Patterns were available for adding ornamental outline stitches, flowers, animals, mottoes, and vignettes such as those by Kate Greenaway, who illustrated children's books. This example of the period contains all these motifs.

While the popularity of crazy quilts peaked in 1884, the *Sewing Machine Advance* noted as late as 1890 that "A crazy quilt is so called because it drives a man nearly crazy when his wife makes one, for it keeps her so busily engaged that she has no time for other work."

Despite such disparagement, crazy patchwork remained popular into the twentieth century. The *Ladies' Home Journal* of January 1904 was still advertising "Embroidery silk for crazy stitches."

SILK CRAZY PATCHWORK

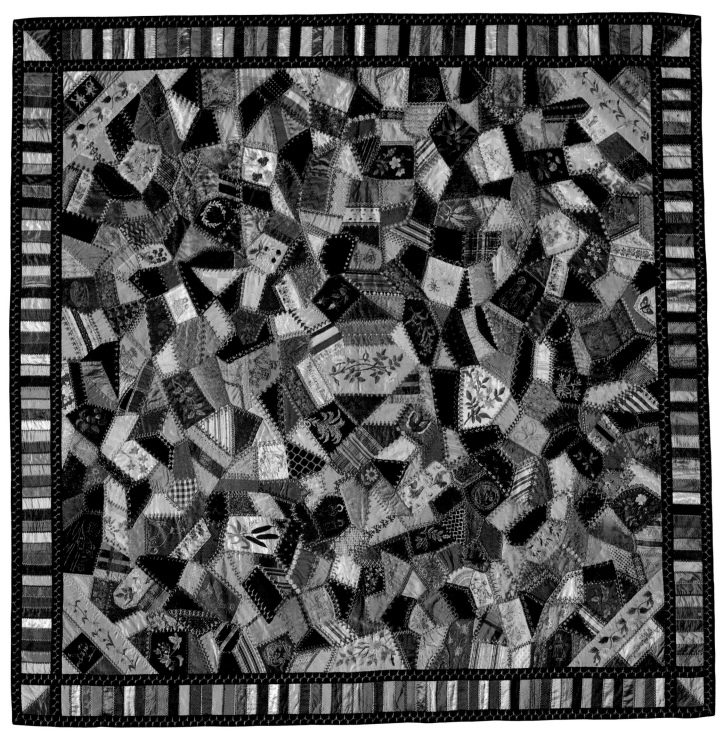

Silk top; silk embroidery, including chenille. Silk lining. Cotton fiber filling.

65 × 65 inches

Cotton top and lining. Cotton fiber filling.

75 × 89 inches

Harriet Powers, an African-American farm woman of Clark County, Georgia, created this lively, subtly balanced expression of her religious fervor. She exhibited her quilt at the Athens Cotton Fair of 1886 where it captured the imagination of Jennie Smith, a young internationally trained local artist. Of her discovery, Jennie later wrote: "I have spent my whole life in the South, and am perfectly familiar with thirty patterns of quilts, but I had never seen an original design, and never a living creature portrayed in patchwork, until the year 1886, when there was held in Athens Georgia, a 'Cotton-Fair,' which was on a much larger scale than an ordinary county fair, as there was a 'Wild West' show, and Cotton Weddings; and a circus, all at the same time. There was a large accumulation of farm products—The largest potatoes, tallest cotton stalk, biggest water-melon! best display of pickles and preserves made by exhibitor! best display of seeds &c and all the attractions usual to such occasions, and in one corner there hung a quilt—which 'captured my eye' and after much difficulty I found the owner. The scenes on the quilt were biblical and I was fascinated. I offered to buy it, but it was not for sale at any price. . . ."

Several years later, Mrs. Powers, at the urging of her husband, because of hard times, offered to sell the quilt for ten dollars, but Miss Smith could then only afford five. Mrs. Powers regretfully turned over her precious creation, but only after providing a description of each section of the design, which Jennie recorded with comments of her own, as follows:

No. 1 represents Adam and Eve in the Garden of Eden, naming the animals, and listening to the subtle whisper of the "sarpent which is degiling Eve." It will be noticed that the only animal represented with feet is the only animal that has no feet. The elephant, camel, leviathan, and ostrich appear in this scene.

No. 2 is a continuation of Paradise but this time Eve has "conceived and bared a son" though he seems to have made his appearance in pantaloons, and has made a pet of the fowl. The bird of Paradise in the right lower corner is resplendent in green and red calico.

No. 3 is "Satan amidst the seven stars," whatever that may mean, and is not as I first thought, a football player. I am sure I have never seen a jauntier devil.

No. 4 is where Cain "is killing his brother Abel, and the stream of blood which flew over the earth" is plainly discernible. Cain being a shepherd is accompanied by sheep.

No. 5 Cain here goes into the land of Nod to get him a wife. There are bears, leopards, elks, and a "kangaroo hog" but the gem of the scene is an orange colored calico lion in the center, who has a white tooth sticking prominently from his lower lip. The leading characteristic of the animal is its large neck and fierce manner. This lion has a tiny neck and a very meek manner and coy expression.

No. 6 is Jacob's dream "when he lied on the ground" with the angel ascending or descending the ladder. She has rather a stylish appearance.

No. 7 is the baptism of Christ. The bat-like creature swooping down is "the Holy Sperret extending in the likeness of a dove."

No. 8 "Has reference to the crucifixion." The globular objects attached to the crosses like balloons by a string represent the darkness over the earth and the moon turning into blood, and is stitched in red and black calico.

No. 9 This is Judas Ascariot and the thirty pieces of silver. The silver is done in green calico. The large disc at his feet is "the star that appeared in 1886 for the first time in three hundred years."

No. 10 is the Last Supper, but the number of disciples is curtailed by five. They are all robed in white spotted cloth, but Judas is clothed in drab, being a little off-color in character.

No. 11 "The next history is the Holy Family; Joseph, the Vargint and the infant Jesus with the stare of Bethlehem over his head. Them is the crosses which he had to bear through his undergoing. Anything for wisement. We can't go back no further than the Bible."

Top of wool and cotton fabrics. Blue cotton lining. Cotton fiber filling.   78 × 73 inches

The quilts made by the Amish people of Pennsylvania, Indiana, and Ohio are visually striking and meticulously crafted. The handsome example above is from the Swarey family of Allenville, Pennsylvania. It was probably made by Mrs. Swarey's grandmother, Mrs. Peachey.

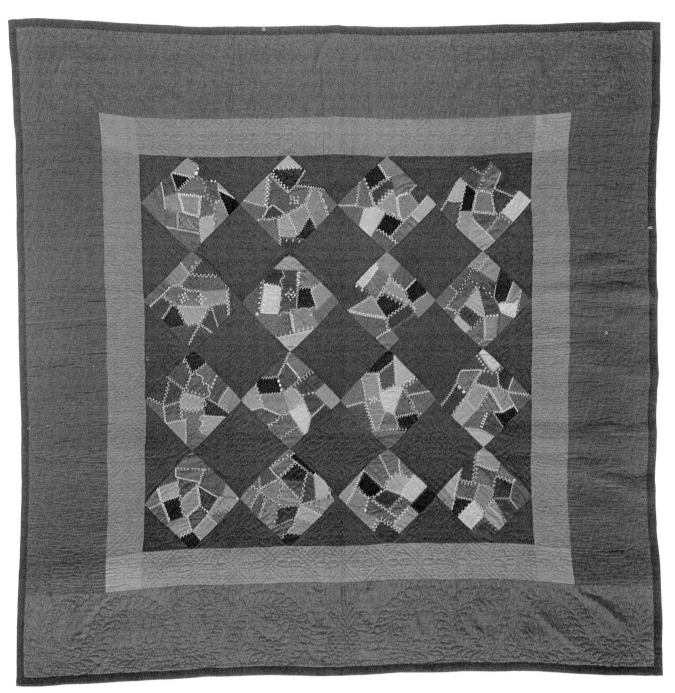

Top of wool and wool-and-cotton fabrics; silk embroidery. Printed cotton lining; initials embroidered in cotton. Cotton fiber filling.

79 × 78 inches

The pieces in the crazy-patch blocks of this Ohio quilt are outlined polychrome silk embroidery in herringbone, feather, buttonhole, thorn, cross, and double-cross stitches. The initials "AK" are embroidered in tan cotton thread on a corner of the lining.

SOLDIER'S BED COVER

Wool.   99 × 99 inches

Needlework in America is largely associated with women, but men are also practitioners of the art, often with notable results. This bed cover was made by Jewett Washington Curtis, and is pieced entirely of 7/8-inch diamonds of wool fabrics, some of which are said to be from Civil War uniforms. The dates 1889 and 1893 appear in the borders. In each corner is an American flag with forty-four stars, the number of states between 1890 and 1896.

Jewett Curtis was born on March 7, 1847 in Montpelier, Vermont, and died on March 20, 1927 in Walcott, New York. He joined the army at the age of fourteen and was discharged with the rank of musician. Returning later as a career soldier, he made this cover while stationed in Alaska. In 1895, he married Mary Ann Putman and they lived on a farm in Mill Plain, Washington.

WOOL CRAZY PATCHWORK

Top of wool fabrics with one piece of silk stitched to a foundation of blue and white cotton ticking; wool and silk embroidery. Wool lining. No filling. 83 × 69 inches

Most of the embroidered patchwork throws of the late nineteenth and early twentieth centuries were made of silk fabrics with silk embroidery. Edna Force Davis of Fairfax County, Virginia, chose wool fabrics and embroidered them in fine wool yarns called "zephyr" because of their lightness and fluffiness. She began the throw in 1897, and finished the crazy patchwork center in the next ten years. Included in the sentimental embroidery motifs are the initials of her daughter, Hazel Louise Davis; her sister-in-law, Amanda Ellen Davis; and a neighbor, Mary Ellen Marshall; music for the opening lines of *Home Sweet*

Home; a symbol of the Odd Fellows fraternity to which her husband belonged; a violin which her husband played; and a reminder that:

> *There is so much good in the worst of us,*
> *And so much bad in the best of us,*
> *That it scarcely behooves any of us,*
> *To talk about the rest of us.*

The border was added in the 1920s, and was embroidered in coarser yarns, because Edna was unable to obtain additional zephyr wools. The two figures in the border represent Edna at the beginning of her endeavor in 1897, and at the end in 1929.

BOTANIST'S QUILT

Silk crazy patchwork stitched to a cotton foundation; silk embroidery, including chenille; a painted motif; silk ribbon appliqué. Silk lining. No filling.

75 × 75 inches

The crazy patchwork of this quilt or parlor throw is divided with black velvet ribbon into nine squares. The outer border is of pink-dotted navy-blue velvet ribbon. Each of the nine squares has a silk square set diagonally in the center and one in each corner (with the exception of one corner of one square), which is embroidered with a beautiful floral motif.

Appropriately, the quiltmaker, Augusta Elizabeth Duvall Bussey, was a botanist. Born in 1843, she lived in Baltimore, Maryland, until her death at the age of eighty-eight.

HAWAIIAN QUILT

Cotton top; cotton, and a small amount of silk, embroidery. Cotton lining. Wool fiber filling.   93 × 91 inches

This quilt was a wedding gift to Rosina Georgetta Kalanikauwekiulani Ayers, who was born on the island of Maui in 1877 and married Dr. Henry Dinegar when she was twenty-one years old. The design consists of four Hawaiian flags and elements from the royal crown and coat of arms. The embroidered figures represent the twin guardians of Hawaii's King Kamehameha I, from whom Rosina Ayers was said to have been descended.

Wool, silk, and cotton top; silk and wool embroidery; silk ribbon trim; penciled details and shading. Cotton lining. No filling.

68 × 67 inches

Although it was not quilted, this needlework cover was called "The Pocahontas Quilt" by the family of Pocahontas Virginia Gay, who made it. Born in Virginia in about 1833, Aunt Poca was a favorite of her nieces and nephews, for whom she made such toys as wax squirrels and birds mounted on tiny pillboxes from the druggist.

White-haired but still erect and slender in the early twentieth century when she made the quilt, she based her designs on popular illustrations of sentimental vignettes and Southern heroes, as well as the Victor dog trademark adopted in 1901 by the Victor Talking Machine Company.

Proud to be a seventh-generation descendant of Pocahontas and John Rolfe, Aunt Poca included a likeness of the Indian princess as she appears in a seventeenth-century engraving frequently reproduced in genealogies.

A similar quilt, made a little later by Pocahontas Virginia Gay, is in the Valentine Museum in Richmond, Virginia.

ABOUT THE QUILTS

QUILTED COUNTERPANE 10

Eve Van Cortlandt, initialled "E V C"; Bronx County, New York; dated 1760.

Quilting; initials and date embroidered in cross-stitch. Quilting: center quatrefoil medallion surrounded by baskets, floral forms, and feathered vines, with a background of diagonal lines 3/16 inch apart. No separate binding; edges of front and lining are turned in and sewn with a running stitch.

Catalogue Number 1979.0184.01

RESIST-DYED QUILT 12

Clara Harrison; Middlebury, Connecticut?; second half, eighteenth century.

Quilting. Quilted in 11-inch-square blocks, with chevrons 3/8 inch apart, emanating from each side of the block and meeting at a point in the center. Binding: straight-grain white cotton strip.

Catalogue Number T. 14268

CHINTZ APPLIQUÉ QUILT TOP 13

Mary Gorsuch Jessop and Cecelia Jessop; Baltimore County, Maryland; center, about 1800; corners added about 1830 or later.

Appliqué; a quilt top only, unfinished.

Catalogue Number T. 15295

SMUGGLER'S QUILT 14

Maker unknown; palampore used as the quilt top probably dates from about 1780. Used in Charleston, South Carolina, and Philadelphia, Pennsylvania. Probably lined and quilted in the mid-nineteenth century.

Quilting. Quilted all over in a diagonal grid. Binding: 3/4-inch woven-patterned cotton tape.

Catalogue Number T. 13945

Gift of Nancy Harper Wheeler

CALIMANCO QUILT 16

Esther Wheat, later Mrs. Benjamin Lee; Conway, Massachusetts; about 1795.

Quilting. Quilting: large feathered heart and two pineapples surrounded by a scrolling vine with large flowers; background filled with diagonal lines 3/8 inch apart; second lining and filling are quilted to the original lining in a 21/2-inch diagonal grid. Binding: straight-grain strip of the red lining fabric machine-stitched to the lining, folded over the edges, and machine-stitched.

Catalogue Number T. 16380

Gift of Olive E. Hurlburt, great-great-granddaughter of Esther Wheat Lee.

REVERSE APPLIQUÉ QUILT 17

M. Campbell; American?; dated 1795.

Pieced work and reverse appliqué; embroidered name and date. Quilting: appliqué is outlined inside and out of edges with one or more rows; white areas around appliqué and pieced border around center are quilted in a diagonal grid; printed-fabric blocks in outer border are alternately quilted in a zigzag pattern, or a horizontal or diagonal grid. Top, bottom, and left side of quilt are bound with linen tape; right side trimmed about 21/2 inches and the edge of the front brought over the lining and whip-stitched.

Catalogue Number 1981.0007.01

BLOCK-PRINTED COTTON QUILT 18

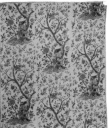

Unknown origin; late eighteenth-century printed cotton, lined and quilted no earlier than the mid-nineteenth century.

Quilting. Quilted all over in a diagonal grid. Binding: 3/4-inch woven-patterned cotton tape.

Catalogue Number T. 16394

Gift of Mr. George Maurice Morris

MARTHA WASHINGTON'S QUILT TOP 20

Martha Washington and Eliza Parke Custis Law; Mount Vernon, Virginia; about 1800–1815.

Pieced work and appliqué; a quilt top only, unfinished.

Catalogue Number 1987. 6019.01

Lent by Mr. Emlyn Marsteller

1812 QUILT 21

Adams family members; Maryland, early nineteenth century.

Pieced work and stuffed work. Quilting: chevron pattern pointing to the center from each side of the pieced blocks; stuffed floral, grape, or feathered circle motifs in each white block; around the border, stuffed feathered vine and flowers, with a background of diagonal lines. Edges of lining are folded over the quilt front and whip-stitched.

Catalogue Number T. 12815

Gift of Mrs. Cecil H. Naylor

FRAMED CENTER QUILT 22

Made by members of the Copp family; Stonington, Connecticut; early nineteenth century.

Pieced work. Quilting: all-over horizontal zigzag lines. Edges of front and lining are turned in and sewn with a running stitch.

Catalogue Number H. 6680

Gift of John Brenton Copp

CHILD'S QUILT 24

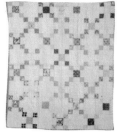

Charlotte Roe; Virgil, New York; dated 1806.

Pieced work; embroidered inscription. Quilting: an eight-pointed star in each block. Right edge of quilt front and lining are turned in and whip-stitched along edge; remaining three edges are bound with stright-grain printed cotton strip, probably a later addition.

Catalogue Number 1984.0092.01

Gift of Ruth Marie Smith

DOUBLE IRISH CHAIN 25

Jane Valentine, later Mrs. Benjamin Brown, Jr.; Scipio, Cayuga County, New York; dated 1825–1830; the date 1832 appears on the lining, probably written in the late nineteenth or early twentieth century by one of Jane Valentine's daughters.

Pieced work in a Double Irish Chain pattern; inked inscriptions. Quilting: diagonal grid following the pieces in the chain; petalled figures in the white blocks. Binding: straight-grain printed-cotton strip.

Catalogue Number E. 287383

Gift of Harriet E. Blodgett

BRITISH SAILOR'S BARTERED QUILT 26

British sailors; before 1820.

Pieced work, appliqué, and embroidery. Unlined; cut edges unbound.

Catalogue Number T. 16356

Lent by Patricia J. Barlow, Mr. Graf's great-great-granddaughter

PRINTED QUILT CENTER 27

Belonged to Mrs. William Alston; near Charleston, South Carolina; about 1830.

Pieced work and appliqué. Quilting: overlapping concentric curves. Binding: cotton tape and straight-grain cotton strips folded over the edges and sewn with a running stitch.

Catalogue Number T. 11666

Gift of Mr. Pinckney Alston Trapier

RISING SUN QUILT 28

Mary "Betsy" Totten; Tottenville, New York, about 1830.

Pieced work and appliqué; embroidered initials, "BT." Quilting: the pieces in the star, and the appliqué in the border are outlined; open spaces in the border are filled with flowers and leaves. Binding: straight-grain printed-cotton strip.

Catalogue Number T. 8153

Gift of Mrs. Marvel Mildred Matthes

GREAT SEAL QUILT 30

Susan Strong; Maryland or Ohio; about 1830.

Appliqué; embroidered details. Quilting: appliqué is outlined; white areas quilted with vines, leaves, and flowers, with feathered bands along the outer edges; double-diagonal grid on blue-ground borders. Binding: edges of the quilt front are folded over the lining and whip-stitched.

Catalogue Number T. 14833

FRANCES M. JOLLY'S QUILT TOP 31

Frances M. Jolly; Massachusetts or North Carolina; dated 1839; the outer border was stitched on later by machine.

Appliqué, embroidery, and braiding. Quilt top only, unfinished.

Catalogue Number 1983.0241.01

Gift of Joy Powell Davis

FORT DEARBORN QUILT 32

Mary Willcox Taylor; Detroit, Michigan; second quarter, nineteenth century.

Pieced work and appliqué with watercolor and embroidery; lining is pieced of square, rectangular, and trapezoidal shapes of blue-and-white striped silk. Quilting: diamond-shaped pieces are outlined; appliquéd and embroidered sections are unquilted. Binding: bias strip of the lining fabric; finished with a woven-and-tied silk fringe.

Catalogue Number T. 11053

Gift of Mrs. John H. Snyder

BRIDE'S QUILT 34

Mary Jane Green Moran; Baltimore, Maryland; about 1846.

Appliqué and embroidery; appliquéd fruit, flowers, and buds are padded; latticework baskets are made of velvet ribbon. Quilt top is quilted to a muslin backing, filling the white background with parallel lines 1/16 to 1/8 inch apart; a rose silk lining is added and the three layers tacked together. Binding: a 5/8-inch white-silk tape is folded over the quilt edges and sewn with a running stitch. Side and bottom edges are finished with a 4 1/2-inch, woven-and-knotted silk fringe.

Catalogue Number 7140

Gift of Kate Carleton Moran Vinson

LOG CABIN AND CIDER QUILT 35

Rebecca Diggs?; Maryland; about 1840.

Appliqué; embroidered details; inked signature "Rebecca Diggs." Quilt top only.

Catalogue Number T. 8755

Gift of Daisy Joseph

ANN'S QUILT 36

Ann, last name unknown; Pittsylvania County, Virginia; probably 1840s.

Appliqué; inked inscription on back. Unlined and unquilted, but with finished edges. Top edge is bound with straight-grain tan cotton strip; side and bottom edges are bound with bias orange cotton strips.

Catalogue Number T. 18124

Gift of Mr. and Mrs. Donald W. Wooster

TOMBSTONE QUILT 37

Nancy Ward Butler; Jamestown, New York; dated 1842.

Appliqué and pieced work. Quilting: diagonal lines in center, a flowering vine around border. Binding: straight-grain white cotton strip.

Catalogue Number T. 18333

Gift of Nancy A. Butler Werdell

MASONIC SYMBOLS QUILT 38

Eliza Rosenkrantz Hussey; Carlisle, Indiana; about 1840.

Pieced work and embroidery; blocks of pieced silk stars and white wool alternating with white wool blocks embroidered with Masonic motifs; embroidered white wool border. Quilting: the blocks with pieced stars have diagonal lines on the stars and diagonal grid on the background; horizontal grid on the embroidered blocks; diagonal lines on the border. Binding: rose silk ribbon.

Catalogue Number 1981.0680.01

Gift of Lucia K. Englehart in memory of her mother, Lucia Knight Kerfoot, Eliza Hussey's granddaughter

ODD FELLOWS QUILT 39

Eliza Rosenkrantz Hussey; Carlisle, Indiana; about 1845.

Pieced work and embroidery; pieced star blocks alternating with embroidered blocks; embroidered border. Quilted all over in a diagonal grid. Binding: straight-grain pink silk strip.

Catalogue Number T. 18877

Lent by Mrs. A. F. Graham

ONE-PATCH PATTERN 40

Laura R. Dwight; Orangeburg, South Carolina; mid-nineteenth-century.

Pieced work, coarsely whip-stitched; flowered chintz border. Quilting: center is tacked at the corners of some of the hexagons; the chintz border is quilted following the main outlines of the printed pattern. Binding: 3/4-inch woven-cotton tape; finished with 4 3/8-inch woven-and-tied cotton fringe.

Catalogue Number T. 17815

Lent by Mrs. H. E. Drought

MULTIPLE PATCH PATTERNS 42

Rachel Burr Corwin; Middle Hope, Orange County, New York; second quarter, nineteenth century.

Pieced work; lining of printed cottons. Much of the quilting follows the pieces, with chains and three- and four-petalled figures filling the larger open spaces. Binding: straight-grain printed cotton strip.

Catalogue Number T. 7118

Gift of Mrs. Daniel Gardner

VANITY OF VANITIES QUILT 43

Emily Holbert; Chester, Orange County, New York; dated 1847.

Appliqué with pieced work sawtooth border. Quilting: appliqué is outlined; quilted veins on the leaves and triple lines on the sashing; background spaces are filled with scrolls, paisley forms, oak leaves, and hearts. Binding: straight-grain printed cotton strip.

Catalogue Number 1988.0245.01

Gift of Mr. and Mrs. John Beard Ecker; Mrs. Ecker is Emily Holbert's grandniece

STUFFED WORK INSCRIPTION 44

Jane Barr; Pennsylvania; dated 1849.

Appliqué; quilted inscription in stuffed work. Quilting: appliqué is outlined; plain blocks are quilted in geometric or floral designs, and one with the inscription; all background quilting is parallel lines 1/4 inch apart. Binding: bias printed cotton strip.

Catalogue Number T. 11101

Gift of Nancy Angeline Ross, Jane Barr's niece

QUAKER ALBUM QUILT 45

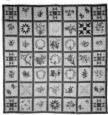

Friends and relatives of Hannah Nicholson; Pennsylvania and New Jersey, dated 1843.

Appliqué, pieced work, and sketching. Inked inscriptions, two surrounded by a stamped floral wreath. Quilted all over in a diagonal grid. No separate binding, edges of the front are folded over the lining and whip-stitched.

Catalogue Number 1986.0657.01

Gift of Thomas B. Grave, Hannah Grave's great-grandson, and his wife

MALTAVILLE ALBUM QUILT 46

Made by members of the Presbyterian Church of Maltaville, New York; other towns named on some of the blocks are Malta, Stillwater, and Clifton Park, all of which are within ten miles of Maltaville; dated April 1847.

Appliqué with embroidered details and inked inscriptions. Quilting: appliqué and block edges are outlined; white background spaces are filled with flowers, leaves, hearts, stars, and crescents, many quilted with double lines; double-lined ovals around many of the signatures. Finished with a 2¼-inch border of straight-grain white cotton seamed all around the quilt front, folded over to the lining and whip-stitched; a piping of printed cotton over cotton cord is set in the top seam.

Catalogue Number T. 6717

Gift of Mrs. Isaac Carrington Morton, granddaughter of the Reverend and Mrs. William Hill

GROOM'S QUILT 48

Friends and family of Benoni Pearce; Pawling, New York; dated 1850.

Appliqué, reverse appliqué, pieced work, and stuffed work; inked and embroidered details and inscriptions. Quilting: overall, the designs are outlined; in the blocks, open spaces contain quilted flowers, leaves, hearts, and circles; in the border, open spaces contain flowers and paired hearts. Binding: straight-grain strip of printed cotton.

Catalogue Number T. 16323

Gift of Adelaide Pearce Green, granddaughter of Benoni Pearce, and her daughter, Mira Pearce Noyes Boorman

SEAMSTRESSES' QUILT 49

Unknown maker; Baltimore, Maryland; mid-nineteenth century.

Appliqué. Quilting: feather plumes in large white spaces; all other spaces are filled by outlining the appliqué and echoing these lines ¼ inch and ⅜ inch apart. Binding: straight edge of red cotton sawtooth border is seamed to the lining, and the serrated edge brought to the front and appliquéd.

Catalogue Number T. 17989

Gift of Doris E. Slothower

ELIZA BAILE'S BRIDE'S QUILT 50

Eliza Jane Baile; Carroll County, Maryland; dated 1850–1851.

Appliqué; embroidered, inked, and watercolored details and inscriptions; strawberries in border are padded with cotton fibers; the berries and cherries in five blocks are sewn on over heavy paper templates. Quilting: appliqué is outlined; double diagonal lines in border and alternating blocks; double-lined grid in remaining blocks. Binding: straight-grain red cotton strip.

Catalogue Number T. 11149

Gift of Addie Baile Manahan

SUNBURST QUILT 52

Anna Sophie Shriver; Funkstown, Maryland; mid-nineteenth century.

Pieced work and stuffed work. Quilting: concentric circles on the pieced circular designs; intervening spaces filled with stuffed feather plumes; stuffed feather vine around border with background of diagonal lines. No separate binding; edges of lining are brought to the front and whip-stitched.

Catalogue Number T. 8433

Gift of Nina Knode Heft

MARYLAND ALBUM QUILT 53

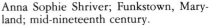

Probably made for a member of the Wilmer family of Kent County, Maryland; about 1840-1860.

Appliqué with embroidered and inked details; signatures are embroidered, inked, and stamped. Quilting: motifs are outlined, with spaces filled by eight-pointed stars, three-leaf clovers, flowers, and leaves. No separate binding; edges of lining are brought to the front and whip-stitched.

Catalogue Number T. 15172

Lent by Mrs. Alan B. Dawson

RUSSELLVILLE FAIR 54

Virginia Ivey; Logan County, Kentucky; about 1856.

Quilting. Quilting: pictorial design in stuffed quilting; background is closely quilted in meandering lines producing a stippled appearance. Bound with 1/2-inch cotton tape; finished with 41/2-inch woven-and-knotted cotton fringe.

Catalogue Number T. 10269

Gift of Miss Lillian V. Lewis

LITTLE SISTER'S QUILT 56

Emily or Susan Holbert; Chester, Orange County, New York; about 1855–60.

Pieced work and appliqué; birds' eyes are worked in blue and black wool buttonhole stitch and the flowers have centers made of sheared yellow wool; the name, S. T. Holbert, is stamped in ink on the lining. Quilting: double outline around all pieced and appliqué motifs; open spaces filled with flowers, running vines, leaves, sprigs, fleurs-de-lys, paisley forms, and hearts, all quilted in double lines. Binding: bias white cotton strip.

Catalogue Number 1988.0245.02

Gift of Mr. and Mrs. John Beard Ecker; Mrs. Ecker is Susan Holbert's granddaughter

STARS AND STRIPES QUILT 57

Mary Rockhold-Teter; Noblesville, Indiana; dated 1861.

Pieced work and appliqué. Quilting: overlapping scallops around border; in the center, rows of overlapping scallops alternate with rows of diagonal grid. Binding: straight-grain red cotton strip.

Catalogue Number T. 8420

Gift of Eugene A. Teter, the grandson of George Teter, and wife, Martha Brown Teter

CIVIL WAR QUILT 58

Mary A. Hughes, later Mrs. Henry Edward Lord; Nashville, Tennessee; about 1860.

Pieced work, with embroidered details and inked signatures. No quilting through all layers, but the red silk lining is machine-quilted to a cotton batting in a diagonal grid. No separate binding; edges of the quilted lining are turned under and whip-stitched to the edges of the ribbon border of the quilt top; finished with a braided red, blue, and gold silk cord.

Catalogue Number T. 8900

Gift of Mary Alice Hughes Lord (deceased) through her children, Rose H. Lord and William Craig Lord

RAISED APPLIQUÉ QUILT 60

Mary and Deborah Palmer; Unadilla Center, Otsego County, New York; mid-nineteenth century.

Appliqué and stuffed work. The appliquéd roses, leaves, and buds are padded with cotton fibers inserted through slashes in the ground fabric, with the petals of the large flowers defined by stitches and individually stuffed; the appliquéd stems are of green cotton fabric wrapped around a roll of white cotton fabric. The stuffed-work basket and two grape wreaths are stitched through the quilt top and a localized backing, and cotton fibers inserted through the backing to raise the pattern. The quilt top is lined and there may be a thin filling of cotton fibers. Through these layers, quilting stitches outline the appliqué and stuffed work. Binding: straight-grain white cotton strip.

Catalogue Number T. 17194-A

Gift of Mr. and Mrs. Kenneth H. Hotchkiss; Mrs. Hotchkiss is the grandniece of Mary and Deborah Palmer

FRUIT AND FLOWERS QUILT 62

Mary Carpenter Pickering, later Mrs. John Bruce Bell; St. Clairsville, Ohio; about 1850–1860.

Appliqué and stuffed work; edges of the appliquéd motifs are covered with fairly close buttonhole stitching; inscription is back-stitched in black silk. All appliquéd motifs are quilted following the designs; plain white blocks and triangles have stuffed work designs; overall background quilting is parallel lines 1/4 inch apart that are horizontal in the quilt center and diagonal in the border. Binding: straight-grain printed cotton strip.

Catalogue Number 1981.0334.01

Gift of Dr. Robert S. Bell in honor of the family of Frank Bell, father of the donor and son of Mary and John Bruce Bell

GARDEN OF EDEN QUILT 63

Probably made by Sylvia S. Queen; Olathe, Kansas; third quarter, nineteenth century.

Pieced work and appliqué, with some of the appliquéd motifs padded; embroidered details. Quilting: the sun, moon, stars, and larger flowers are outlined, and some also quilted in a fine grid; background is quilted in parallel lines 3/8 inch apart. Scalloped edge is bound with bias printed cotton strip that is both hand- and machine-stitched.

Catalogue Number T. 15534

Gift of Dorothy Diffey Bledsoe in memory of her grandmother, Laura Doty Diffey

MACHINE QUILTING 64

Unknown origin; about 1860.

Machine and hand quilting; stuffed and corded work. Quilting: each block has a different motif, each triangle around the edges has a leafy sprig. Right and bottom edges have original binding, a 3/4-inch twill-weave cotton tape; bottom edge has a 1 1/2-inch extension of white cotton fabric enclosing the binding; top and left edges appear to have been cut by about 4 1/4 inches and bound with bias cotton strip.

Catalogue Number T. 18240

Gift of Mr. and Mrs. Samuel Schwartz

CHRISTMAS TREE QUILT 66

Susan Rogers; Brooklyn, New York; dated 1867.

Appliqué and embroidery. Quilting: design in each block is outlined, with backgrounds in curved lines, circles, diagonal lines, diagonal grid, wave, chain, or shell patterns. Binding: straight-grain tan cotton.

Catalogue Number T. 15474

Gift of Eva McNeill

SOLAR SYSTEM QUILT 68

Ellen Harding Baker; Iowa; dated 1876.

Appliqué, embroidery, and braiding. Quilting: the sun is quilted in a diagonal grid surrounded by a feathered circle; between the orbits of the planets are feathered bands and shell quilting; the outer edges are shell-quilted with a feathered circle in each of the lower corners. Binding: straight-grain red twill-weave wool.

Catalogue Number 1983.0618.01

Gift of Patricia Hill McCloy and Kathryn Hill Meardon, granddaughters of Ellen Harding Baker

FAMILY VIGNETTE 69

Unknown maker; Ulster County, New York; probably third quarter, nineteenth century.

Appliqué with embroidered details. Unlined. Edged with appliquéd scallops, the straight edges of which are seamed to the edge of the counterpane, and the rounded edges turned under and appliquéd to the ground fabric with a running stitch.

Catalogue Number T. 17737

CHESTNUT BURR TABLE COVER 70

Made by donor's grandmother, name unknown; Earlville, Illinois; about 1860.

Pieced work with embroidery. Each block is pieced on a muslin foundation, with paper templates still in place; between each piece and its template is a thin layer of cotton fiber filling. No quilting. Binding: a 5/8-inch-wide border of bias black velvet is stitched to the foundation muslin, and the edges of the pieced work and lining are turned under and whip-stitched to the velvet.

Catalogue Number T. 10972

Gift of Chester Wells Clark

PARLOR QUILT 71

Unknown origin; second half, nineteenth century.

Pieced work and chenille embroidery. Quilting through the pieced work, its filling, and its lining: all hexagons and diamonds are outlined. Quilting through the red silk underside, its filling, and its lining: running feather, feather circles, and diagonal grid. Binding: a green silk covered cord is stitched to the black velvet border; a machine-pleated red silk ribbon is attached to the edges of the red silk quilt and are whipped to the back of the green cord.

Catalogue Number T. 12917

Gift of Stewart Dickson

OCEAN WAVE QUILT 72

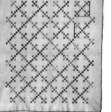

Mary Ann Bishop; Wilkesville, Vinton County, Ohio; about 1875.

Pieced work. Quilting: straight lines on pieced sections; feathered circles on the plain cotton centers; feathered leaves, using template, and diagonal lines on the border. Binding: straight edge of red cotton sawtooth border is seamed to the lining, and the serrated edge brought to the front and appliquéd.

Catalogue Number T. 7851

Gift of Miss Maude M. Fierce

DOUBLE NINE-PATCH QUILT 73

Mary Ann Bishop; Wilkesville, Vinton County, Ohio; mid-nineteenth century.

Pieced work. Quilting: diagonal lines on pieced blocks, diagonal grid on plain squares; feathered leaf, using templates, and diagonal lines on the borders and the plain rectangles between the pieced blocks. Binding: straight edge of printed blue cotton sawtooth border is seamed to the lining, and the serrated edge appliquéd to the front.

Catalogue Number T. 7850

Gift of Miss Maude M. Fierce

CENTENNIAL-PRINT COTTON QUILT 74

Emily Bradbury, Harriet Bradbury, and Maria Robertson; Charlestown, New Hampshire; about 1876.

Pieced work top and lining. Randomly quilted in diagonal lines, straight lines, diagonal grid, and chevrons. Binding: straight-grain printed cotton strip.

Catalogue Number T. 10090

Gift of Mrs. C. A. Rich (Harriet Bradbury)

NURSE'S QUILT 76

Betty West; Washington, D.C.; about 1879.

Pieced work; a quilt top only, unfinished.

Catalogue Number T. 17773-A

Gift of Mr. and Mrs. Kennedy C. Watkins

STATES AND TERRITORIES BED COVER 77

Maker unknown; Washington, D.C.; dated 1883–1884.

Pieced work, appliqué, embroidery, and hand-painting; not quilted or tied. Edges of the plush border are turned to the back and the lining whipped to it; a heavy red and gold silk cord is whipped to the folded edge of the plush.

Catalogue Number T. 13234

Gift of the Louise Home

SILK CRAZY PATCHWORK 78

Maker unknown; about 1885.

Pieced work and embroidery. Not quilted, but tied every 5 inches through all layers with pink and green silk yarns. Edges of the pale green satin lining are brought to the front and whip-stitched.

Catalogue Number T. 11233

Gift of Mrs. Thomas J. White

BIBLE QUILT 80

Harriet Powers; vicinity of Athens, Georgia; about 1886.

Pieced work and appliqué, hand- and machine-stitched. Quilting: outline around motifs and random intersecting straight lines in open spaces. A 1-inch border of straight-grain printed cotton (the same fabric used in the bird of paradise) is folded over the edges and machine-stitched through all layers.

Catalogue Number T. 14713

Gift of Mr. and Mrs. H. M. Heckman

AMISH QUILT 82

Mrs. Peachey; Allenville, Mifflin County, Pennsylvania; late nineteenth or early twentieth century.

Pieced work. Quilting: eight-pointed stars and/or grid in the squares; shell in the triangles; diagonal lines in the horizontal bands; vines with leaves in the side and bottom borders. Top and bottom edges bound with violet, straight-grain wool-and-cotton; side edges bound with straight-grain pink satin-weave cotton.

Catalogue Number T. 18479

AMISH QUILT 83

"AK"; Ohio; first third, twentieth century.

Pieced work and embroidery. Quilting: feathered circles with diagonal-grid centers in the blue squares; four-petalled figures or pumpkin seeds on the sides, and eight-pointed stars in the corners of the inner border; each outer border, scrolling feathered vines with a pineapple at the center. Binding: straight-grain red wool strip.

Catalogue Number 1985.0029.06

Gift of Mrs. Robert B. Stephens

SOLDIER'S BED COVER 84

Jewett Washington Curtis; Alaska; dated 1889–1893.

Pieced work. Unlined and unbound.

Catalogue Number 1984.0406.01

Gift of Mr. Clark E. Curtis, son of Jewett Washington Curtis

WOOL CRAZY PATCHWORK 85

Edna Force Davis; Fairfax County, Virginia; dated 1897–1929.

Pieced work and embroidery; the pieced work is stitched to an interlining of blue-and-white ticking. No quilting, but a vertical line of stitching every 10 inches holds the lining to the ticking; the stitches do not go through the pieced work. Edges are finished with a 2-inch border of blue straight-grain twill-weave wool.

Catalogue Number T. 13779

Gift of Hazel Davis, daughter of Edna Force Davis

BOTANIST'S QUILT 86

Augusta Elizabeth Duvall Bussey; Baltimore, Maryland; late nineteenth century.

Pieced work and embroidery. Quilting: both edges of the velvet-ribbon frames around the blocks as well as the inner border of the border are outlined. Binding: straight-grain mauve silk strip.

Catalogue Number T. 13517

Gift of Marion H. Phelps, H. Lee Hoffman, and Charles Hoffman, grandniece and grandnephews of Augusta Bussey

HAWAIIAN QUILT 87

Maker unknown; Hawaii; about 1898.

Pieced work, appliqué, and embroidery. Quilting: in the center, the background is filled by outlining the motifs and echoing these lines 1 inch apart; the Union Jacks are quilted in chevron patterns emanating from the sides and corners, with those from the sides meeting at a point in the center; the white stripes are quilted in chevrons, the blue stripes in diagonal lines, and the red stripes in a diagonal grid. Binding: on-the-grain red cotton strip, both hand- and machine-stitched.

Catalogue Number T. 18486

Gift of Adelaide D. McDonough, daughter of Rosina Dinegar

POCAHONTAS QUILT 88

Pocahontas Virginia Gay; Fluvanna County, Virginia; early twentieth century.

Appliqué, pieced work, and embroidery; pencilled or inked details and shading. No quilting. Bound with black wool braid folded over the edges and machine-stitched through all layers.

Catalogue Number T. 11694

Gift of Mrs. Edward McGarvey, wife of Pocahontas Gay's grandnephew

ACKNOWLEDGMENTS

American Quilts was conceived, developed, and produced by Gramercy Books and the Book Development Division, Smithsonian Institution Press.

Gramercy Books: Glorya Hale, Editorial Director; Frank Finamore, Assistant Editor; Jamila Miller, Designer; Ellen Reed, Production Supervisor.

Book Development Division, Smithsonian Institution Press: Caroline Newman, Executive Editor; Paula Ballo Dailey, Picture Editor; Heidi Lumberg, Assistant Editor.

Special thanks to Grace Rogers Cooper, Rita Adrosko, and the Division of Textiles staff and volunteers, Robert D. Selim, and the Office of Printing and Photographic Services.

Portrait of Eve Van Cortlandt, p. 10, courtesy of the Van Cortlandt Museum, Bronx, New York.